Japanese Healthy, High-Style Cooking

Front Cover Photo:
Japanese Salmon Dinner
page 42

Published by Triangle Park Press

Copyright © 1998 by Sumiko Matsumoto all rights reserved.
No part of this book may be reproduced in any form or by any means without permission except that passages may be quoted in critical articles and reviews.

Printed in the United States of America
First Edition 1999
"Library of Congress Catalog Card Number" 98-61067
Author Matsumoto Sumiko
Japanese Healthy, High-Style Cooking

Includes bibliographical references and index

ISBN 0-9666131-0-4
U.P.C. Manufacturer Code I D number 662262

Copy edited by Alice K. Donahue
Proofread by Shirlee Gates
Front Cover Photo: Salmon Dinner (Japanese)

Japanese Healthy, High-Style Cooking:

Step-by-Step Winning Recipes
as used in
Lake Forest, Illinois
La Jolla and Palm Springs, California
and
Boca Raton, Florida

By
Chef
Sumiko Matsumoto

Triangle Park Press
Lake Forest, Illinois

I dedicate this book to the people of my church
who prayed with me and kept the faith for me.
I pray this book is worthy of your trust.

Table of Contents

Acknowledgments 11
Introduction 13
Recipes Approach 16
Shopping Tips 18
Japanese Dinners 23
        (See photos on pages 25 and 26.)
Sushi 27-29
Beef Teriyaki Dinner 30
Chicken Teriyaki with Vegetables and Rice Dinner 31
Chicken and Vegetable Stir Fry 32-33
Chop Cher Dinner 34-35
Japanese Style Meat and Vegetable Dinner 36-37
Japanese Style Orange Roughy and Vegetables Dinner ... 38-39
Pork Tenderloin and Vegetable Wok Cooking Dinner 40-41
Salmon Dinner 42-43
Shish-Kabobs with Japanese Rice Dinner 44-45
Shrimp Egg Roll Dinner 46-47
Shrimp Fried Rice Dinner 48-49
Shrimp Tempura Dinner 50-51
Shrimp Vegetable Dinner 52-53
Stuffed Japanese Brown Mushroom Dinner 54-55
Whitefish Dinner with Red and Yellow Peppers 56-57
Japanese Style Vegetable Dinner 58
Sukiyaki Dinner 59

Japanese Soup and Vegetables 61
Miso Soup 63
Bok Choy 64
Japanese White Rice 65
Japanese White Rice with Red Japanese Beans 66
Mixed Vegetables 67
Renkon (Lotus Root) 68
Yam Cakes 69
        (See photos on pages 71 and 72.)

American Dinners 73
Barbecue Dinner. 75
Baby Beef Liver Dinner. 76-77
Beef Loaf Dinner 78
Capon Dinner. 79
Chicken Drumettes 80-81
Chicken Vegetable Roll Dinner. 82-83
Chicken Casserole Dinner 84
Chicken Dinner 85
Fresh Ham Dinner 86-87
Fresh Vegetable Deep Dish Pizza Dinner 88-89
Fresh Vegetable Stew Dinner. 90-91
Golden Tilapia Fillets Dinner 92-93
Fish Dinner. 94
Leg of Lamb Dinner 95
Lobster Dinner 96
Pork Tenderloin with Sweet Potatoes Dinner 97
Red Snapper 98
Roast Beef Dinner 99
Roast Pork Tendcrloin Dinner 100
Salmon Casserole Dinner 101
Scallops Dinner. 102-103
Shrimp Pasta Dinner 104-105
Spaghetti with Tomato Sauce Dinner 106-107
Salmon Dinner. 108
Veal Cutlet Dinner. 109

Soups. 111
Basic Chicken Stock 113
Carrot Soup 114
Chicken Vegetable Soup 115
Corn Soup. 116
Fifteen Bean Soup. 117
Mushroom Soup. 118
Spinach Soup 119
Split Green Pea Soup 120

American Vegetables 121
Acorn Squash 123
American Brown Rice 124
American Wild Rice 125
Asparagus 126
Asparagus Appetizer 127
Baby Beets 128
Baby Carrots 129
Baby New Potatoes in Jackets 130
Baked Baby New Potatoes in Jackets 131
Baked Potatoes 132
Broccoli 133
Brussels Sprouts 134
Green Beans 135
Lima Beans 136
Oven Fried Potato Cubes 137
Pearl Onions 138
Peas 139
Sweet Potatoes 140
Spinach Vegetable Dish 141
Tomato Slices 142
Yellow Squash and Zucchini 143

Lunch Salads 145
Sumiko's Special Salad Dressing 147
Apple Salad with Squash 148-149
Broccoli Salad 150-151
Chicken Salad 152-153
Chicken Fruit Salad 154-155
Egg Salad 156-157
New Red Potato Salad 158-159
Salmon Salad 160-161
Shrimp Vegetable Salad 162-163
Spinach Salad 164
Vegetable Salad 165
Tuna Salad 166-167

Desserts—Light and Quick 169
Applesauce 171
Baked Apples 172
Baked Peaches 173
Fresh Baked Apple Pie 174-175
Fresh Cranberry Sauce. 176
Fresh Fruit and Jell-O® Mold 177
Fresh Fruit Dessert. 178
Ice Cream, Peanut Butter and
    Honey Graham Cracker Dessert 179
Oatmeal Raisin Cookies 180
Steamed Pears 181
Stewed Fresh Fruit. 182

Index to Recipes 185-190
Order Form. 191

Acknowledgments

I am truly indebted to Joyce Ekdahl for taking my recipes and transcribing them. Her patience and guidance were a godsend.

Diana Hampson did the word processing for publishing. She wore many hats during the preparation of this book. Thank you, Diana.

Curt Hampson shepherded the project from idea to reality. Curt is truly a gifted man.

Mary Beth Jones, President First Chicago Bank, Lake Forest, and her staff tasted many of the recipes in this book. Her critical acclaim was key to many recipes.

I appreciate the support I received from my daughter Lynda. I often turned to Lynda when the going was tough, and she was always there with love.

Introduction

Sumiko Matsumoto, a Japanese American, is a successful cook for an exclusive clientele in select settings in this country: Lake Forest, Illinois—north of Chicago on Lake Michigan; La Jolla and Palm Springs in California; and Boca Raton in Florida. Over the years she has developed a winning mix of Japanese and American recipes to please this select but diverse group. This book tells the story of her venture into the American palate, pleasing some of the most exacting gourmets on both coasts and in between. A key to her success is her ability to judge a client's taste, cater to it, and, yet, introduce, by stages, Japanese flavors and culinary experiences.

Central to her method is *simplicity*—an almost Zen-like commitment to the essence of things. She emphasizes using the freshest ingredients, subtle seasonings, and a lightness of touch that is very much in step with Americans' consciousness of a healthy diet.

This book contains not only Japanese recipes for Americans, but also traditional American dishes interpreted through Sumiko's method. Through this process, she re-introduces discerning Americans to old standards.

Many of Sumiko's clients urged her to share the recipes which brought her catering into such demand. Yet, it is not the recipes alone, but also the philosophy she espouses which is conveyed here—a rediscovery of the traditional respect for food including ingredients, preparation, and presentation.

This emphasis on diet and the social experience of mealtime is timely. Americans approaching the millennium are rediscovering the values of shared family meals and of cultivating friendships, even global ones, through special shared repasts. In the nineteenth century, as rail and steamship travel brought Europe closer for Americans, a new generation discovered the French reverence for both cuisine and the social experience of a special meal together. French restaurants sprang up in major cities and French cuisine was a mark of cosmopolitan style. The French way of life was an overdue antidote to the traditional Puritan simplicity in all things, including food and mealtimes. But, American get-up-and-go really never has been synonymous with the two-hour lunch of single-dish courses, wines at each "stop," and rich sauces. This societal contrast, French to American, is capsulated in one paraphrased comment of a recent French first minister, "Who cares if our cars are a bit below world-class, if we still can have our two-hour lunches!"

Indeed, the French approach uses rich sauces and goes well with wine, neither of which are conducive to returning to a busy work day after lunch or even to everyday after supper activities in the home. The Japanese, as we know, have both excellent cuisine and good cars. That's what most Americans want: a better American cuisine consistent with their highly-productive way of living. Today, once again, a travel-speed revolution has brought every corner of the world within easy access of a great many people. This new world-conscious, travel-broadened American public is ready for a new approach to mealtime, which combines renewed attention to the art and craft of cooking while respecting the health and schedule imperatives of what Anthony Trollope called "The way we live now." The Japanese approach offers some of the best of the French approach: the traditional respect for ingredients, presentation, and taste, while also addressing today's concerns about health and post-meal activity. The Japanese approach, then, offers light, healthful, tasty meals just when Americans are most open to this suggestion.

Sumiko's contribution, then, has been to bring this timely and pertinent style of cooking to a discerning, busy, cosmopolitan audience. Her recipes presented here offer accessible, replicable step-by-step guides to recreating a traditional dining experience which fits perfectly into our modern lifestyle.

Recipes Approach

Growing up in Japan, Sumiko often accompanied her mother when she went about choosing the food for her family. Her mother loved to select her capons and would always make sure the bird was healthy, with a plump feeling and well-rounded breast, clear of any skin blemishes and bruising. She would then take the bird home and rinse it well in cold water and dry it with a clean towel. She also picked the vegetables according to the season with an eye for pleasing color and flavors which enhanced the tasty bird she was preparing. She made sure the bird was cooked in a moderate oven and removed at the right time to ensure maximum flavor and proper color and texture. Her focus was on preparing the bird to suit her family and her guests. Indeed, Sumiko's capon recipes here are all adapted from her mother's traditional methods.

When Sumiko was given the opportunity to prepare food for people in Lake Forest, Illinois, she went about it in the manner learned from her mother. She has always worked to please her clients and to develop a menu range which would both educate and diversify the client's palate. In the privileged setting of Chicago's north shore, she found that clients were accustomed to fine food, artistically prepared. Also, this setting allowed Sumiko to conduct her shopping expeditions in markets well-stocked with fresh produce, fresh highly-graded meats, and fresh fish. Sumiko knew that the only way to control the flavor and quality of her recipes was to insist on fresh ingredients. She was also able to find the variety which enabled her to pick complementary colors for each entree.

Colorful foods, such as her sushi recipe here, are versatile: they can be served as a meal, an appetizer, or a snack.

Japanese green tea is always served first. Tea is prepared by filling a strainer with Japanese green tea and pouring boiling water through the strainer into the teapot. This method assures the tea will be delicate. Like French wine, tea is a symbol of convivial hospitality and is placed into the hands of the guest from the start.

Fresh ingredients, savvy preparation, and an eye to presentation and hospitality all set up this Japanese way of cooking as an ideal cuisine for Americans in the new millennium. As a reaction against prepared, hackneyed and dubiously healthful fast food and easy preparation norms today, Sumiko's Japanese approach offers a new way of living as well as cooking.

The fresh ingredients, too, avoid additives such as sugar and sodium.

Shopping — The First Step in Good Cooking

Introduction

After menu planning, shopping begins the real craft of cooking. It cannot be rushed, and the cook who would be successful needs to clear a time in the schedule to shop when not harried or preoccupied. Find out from your grocer when the new items for the weekend are available. As a general rule, Thursdays and during the day offer the best selections. When shopping for a special occasion, for instance a Saturday night dinner party, taking the extra effort to shop early on that day to get the freshest ingredients can improve the quality of the meal.

Meat, Poultry and Fish

The butcher who knows you and knows your standards without having to ask will respect your expectations for quality and freshness. It follows, then, that discerning cooks will avoid purchasing frozen meats, poultry, and fish so the marked difference in taste can thus be avoided.

Chicken and Turkey

Choose a whole bird with a plump, well-rounded breast and with clear skin free of blemishes and bruising. Skin color, though, may vary from white to yellow according to what the bird was fed and is not an indication of quality. Depending on feeds expect to find whiter flesh in spring and summer and more yellow meat in fall and winter.

Pork

Choose meat which has a high proportion of lean to fat and avoid both masses of fat and bits of bone. Leaner, expensive cuts of pork will yield a surprisingly high quantity of edible portions. The fat should be solid and white and the lean meat firm and finely-textured, with a grayish-pink to light-red color.

Beef

Beef should be of a uniform, bright color. The texture of the meat should be fine rather than coarse, firm and slightly moist, and the bones should be white and porous. The color of the fat is not indicative of quality. Some beef is aged to increase its tenderness. Note that beef which has been tenderized by aging will not require further tenderizing before cooking.

Lamb

Meat of a young sheep should be pink to light red in color, firm and fine textured. The bone should be white with a pink center. The color of the fat is not an indication of quality. Always choose lamb which has a high proportion of leaner meat to masses of fat and bone.

Fish

Fresh fish is a delight to smell. If it smells less than delightful, or fishy, this is an indication that it is not fresh. Look for full, bright eyes, healthy pink gills, and firm texture. Buy a whole fish and ask the butcher to fillet it for you.

Salad Ingredients and Vegetables

Similar to cultivating a knowledgeable butcher, get to know your produce persons and, if possible, ask for access to the newest arrivals often found in the back of the store. At Don's Finest Foods in Lake Forest, Illinois, for instance, a long-standing relationship has enabled the author to obtain the very freshest items.

Economizing—Priorities and Pitfalls

As noted earlier, the best values go to the early shoppers so getting to the market first helps stretch dollars. In general, once you are there, prioritize quality over quantity.

In meats, shift from expensive lamb, beef, and salmon to chicken, pork, and whitefish. In winter, avoid certain scarcer vegetables such as peppers. Instead, prepare a mixture of broccoli, carrots and mushrooms or serve canned or frozen petite peas or beets. For salads, the cheapest ingredient is always head lettuce. Also, fruits to be used in the winter can include oranges, apples, and occasionally melons. The more fragile berries out of season will be more costly, reflecting their delicate handling.

Choosing Markets—Starting Out With An Advantage

The Japanese way of cooking utilizes the best fresh ingredients from a variety of good sources. For example, in Lake Forest, Illinois, Sumiko trusts and respects Don's Finest Foods' approach—seeking out from Don's store the freshest meats and vegetables which he procures from the Chicago central market at Fulton Street very early each morning. But, in general, the Yaohan chain of

Japanese markets, headquartered in Tokyo, has several outlets in major centers around the United States which are worth seeking out for the freshest ingredients. Shigeki Takimoto, manager at Yaohan's in Arlington Heights, Illinois, markets fresh meats and vegetables for the discerning cook. Following is a list of Yaohan markets, which are mostly concentrated in California, although outlets can be found in Chicago and New York.

California:

333 South Alameda Street, Los Angeles, CA 90013. Telephone: 213-687-6699.
21515 Western Avenue, Torrance, CA 90501. Telephone: 310-782-0335. Fax: 310-782-0846.
665 Paularino Avenue, Costa Mesa, CA 92626. Telephone 714-557-6699. Fax: 714-557-6342
515 West Las Tunas Drive, San Gabriel, CA 91776. Telephone: 818-457-2899. Fax: 818-457-2893.
3760 Centinela Avenue, Los Angeles, CA 90066. Telephone: 310-398-2113. Fax: 310-398-8320.
675 Saratoga Avenue, San Jose, CA 95129. Telephone: 408-255-6699. Fax: 408-255-5108.
4240 Kearny Mesa Road, #119, San Diego, CA 92111. Telephone: 619-569-6699. Fax: 619-569-8060.

Chicago Area:

100 East Algonquin Road, Arlington Heights, IL 60005. Telephone: 847-956-6699. Fax: 847-956-6776.

New York Area:

595 River Road, Edgewater, NJ 07020. Telephone: 201-941-9113. Fax: 201-941-5437.

Japanese Dinners

Beef Teriyaki Dinner
Page 30

Chicken Teriyaki with Vegetables and Rice Dinner
Page 31

Chop Cher Dinner
Page 34

Japanese Style Vegetable Dinner
Page 58

Salmon Dinner
Page 42

Shrimp Tempura Dinner
Page 50

Wood tub for cooling rice.

Fillet mignon, spinach, pollock, radish.

Tossing rice and adding vinegar to cool.

Spreading rice on top of the seaweed.

Add fillet mignon, spinach, pollock, and radish. Roll bamboo sheet away from you.

Cut rolls crosswise into 1" to 1-1/2" sections. Place cut side up.

Sushi

Japanese style cooking calls for many ingredients readily available at your larger grocery stores and at specialized Japanese markets.

Serves four.

Sushi is a Japanese, artistic, decorative, and popular contribution to the field of cooking. It can be made of fish, shrimp, or meat with rice in colorful and appetizing arrangements. This recipe is just one example.

Utensils:

Bamboo sheet
18" x 24" cutting board
Medium pot with tight lid for cooking rice
Strainer for washing rice
Bowl for marinating meat
11" frying pan
13" bowl for cooling rice
Bamboo spatula or wooden spoon, dampened
Bowl for dipping

Ingredients:

2 cups Japanese rice
1/2 cup rice vinegar
1 pound package thinly sliced filet mignon
6 ounce package of cooked pollock
1 package Japanese pickled yellow radish
2 bundles fresh spinach
Teriyaki marinade and sauce
Lite soy sauce
Sesame oil
Sweet cooking rice wine

Fresh ginger, 2-inch piece
Roasted sesame seeds
White pepper
One package of ten seaweed sheets
One ounce can of dry horseradish (optional)
2 packages yam cakes (optional)

Rice:

Rinse two cups of rice until water is clear. Drain. Cook according to package directions. When done, place in the 13-inch bowl. Toss and fan until cool (about 10 minutes). While the rice is just warm, add the rice vinegar a little at a time while tossing. Set aside.

Meat Marinade:

1/4 cup teriyaki marinade and sauce
1 teaspoon lite soy sauce
1 tablespoon sesame oil
1 teaspoon sweet cooking rice wine
1 tablespoon fresh ginger, peeled and finely chopped
1 teaspoon roasted sesame seeds
1/4 teaspoon white pepper

Mix the ingredients for the marinade. Place the meat in the marinade for 3 - 4 minutes. Drain the meat. In the frying pan, warm one tablespoon of sesame oil. Add the meat and sauté until light brown. Strain the beef over a bowl. Set aside.

Spinach:

Wash and remove the stems leaving the leaves whole. Steam in their own moisture one minute. Rinse quickly in cold water to preserve color. Pat dry. Set aside.

JAPANESE DINNERS

Cut cooked pollock and Japanese pickled yellow radish in chop stick size strips and set aside.

Preparation of sushi:

Rinse the bamboo sheet in cold water and shake off excess. Place on a cutting board. Mix one tablespoon of sesame seed oil and one cup of cold water in the dipping bowl. Dip fingers into dipping bowl when working. Place one sheet of seaweed on top of the bamboo sheet. Place 2 - 3 tablespoons of rice in the center of the sheet. Spread to within three inches of each end. Place one layer of the filet mignon on top of the rice, saving enough for the other nine rolls. Place three leaves of spinach over the meat. Place one strip of pollock on the spinach, saving enough for the other nine rolls. Place one strip of Japanese pickled yellow radish on each roll. Roll the bamboo sheet away from you, pressing tightly and smoothly as you roll. Unroll bamboo sheet and remove Sushi. Prepare the rest of the rolls. Let the rolls rest for five minutes before cutting. Using a sharp wet knife, cut each rice roll crosswise into 1 - 1-1/2 inch sections. Turn the cut side up to show the design of the food.

Serving suggestion:

Serve with one tablespoon of the horseradish powder mixed with water and stirred until very thick. Serve lite soy sauce in small individual bowls for dipping. Yam cakes may be served as a vegetable. Rinse in cold water, halve, and cut in slices. Serve cold.

Beef Teriyaki Dinner

Serves four.

Ingredients:

2 - 3 pounds beef, filet mignon, sliced about 1/4 inch thick
2 medium cloves of garlic, chopped
1 inch piece fresh ginger, peeled and chopped
1/4 cup sesame seed oil
1 teaspoon toasted sesame seeds
1/4 teaspoon black pepper
1/4 teaspoon salt
1 tablespoon sweet cooking rice wine
1/3 cup teriyaki marinade and sauce
1/4 cup lite soy sauce
1 tablespoon pure honey
1 large onion, chopped

Preparation:

Wash the meat and pat dry. Mix all other ingredients in an 11 inch mixing bowl. Add the meat and marinate. Cover and refrigerate until ready to use. Preheat broiler on broil for 10 minutes. Drain the meat. Line the broiler tray with aluminum foil and add the meat. Broil for 3 - 4 minutes on each side. Keep the broiler open about one inch while cooking.

Serving suggestion:

Serve with Japanese rice and zucchini with red pepper strips for a colorful side dish.

JAPANESE DINNERS

Chicken Teriyaki with Vegetables and Rice Dinner

Teriyaki means "shining broil."
Serves four.

Ingredients:

    2 whole boneless, skinless chicken breasts, split for 4 servings
    4 boneless, skinless chicken thighs
    1/2 cup teriyaki marinade and sauce
    1/3 cup lite soy sauce
    1/4 cup Japanese sweet cooking rice wine
    1 tablespoon sesame seed oil
    3 large cloves of garlic, finely chopped
    1 tablespoon pure honey
    1 inch piece fresh ginger, peeled and finely chopped
    1/2 teaspoon black pepper
    1/4 teaspoon salt
    1 medium onion, coarsely sliced
    1 teaspoon toasted sesame seeds

Preparation:

Wash chicken and pat dry. Mix remaining ingredients except onion and cover the chicken with the marinade sauce. Refrigerate covered until ready to use. Drain the sauce from the chicken and reserve. Preheat broiler for 10 minutes on broil. Place the chicken in the bottom of the broiler pan. Place the broiler pan in the middle of the broiler tray. Broil the chicken for 4 - 5 minutes on each side. When turning to second side, brush with reserved sauce. Add the onion and broil 4 - 5 minutes. Pour broiler juices over chicken before serving.

Chicken and Vegetable Stir Fry Dinner

Serves four.

Ingredients:

2 pounds boneless, skinless chicken breasts
2 stalks leeks
1 cup bamboo shoots
5 petite Japanese eggplants
1/3 pound Chinese pea pods
1 bunch spinach
1/2 pound Japanese bean sprouts
1/2 pound Shiitake mushrooms
3 carrots (choose bright orange carrots with green tops)
2 garlic cloves
2 inches ginger
1/4 cup Japanese cooking wine
1/2 teaspoon black pepper
1/2 teaspoon salt
1/3 cup sesame oil
1/3 cup teriyaki marinade and sauce
1/4 cup lite soy sauce

Preparation:

Wash chicken, pat dry, remove all fat, diagonally slice and place in a mixing bowl. Add soy sauce and teriyaki sauce. Peel garlic and one inch of the ginger, chop very fine, and add to the chicken. Add salt, pepper, one tablespoon sesame oil and one tablespoon Japanese cooking wine. Mix thoroughly, cover, and refrigerate until ready to use. Wash all vegetables and pat dry. Remove tops and bottoms from leeks. Remove tops and bottoms and peel carrots. Remove bottoms from spinach. Diagonally cut carrots, leeks, and bamboo shoots. Dice Japanese eggplants. Cut tips off mushroom stems. Remove tops and bottoms from China peas. Peel and slice one inch of the ginger.

Pour one tablespoon sesame oil into wok, place on high heat. Add leeks, eggplants, and bamboo shoots, stir and cook for one minute, remove to a warm dish. Pour one tablespoon sesame oil into wok, place on high heat. Add carrots, mushrooms, and China peas, stirring continuously. Stir in spinach, bean sprouts and ginger, cook for one minute. Turn off heat. Add leeks, eggplants, and bamboo shoots. Mix thoroughly. Add to warm serving plate, keep warm. Place wok on high heat, add chicken with marinade sauce, stir while cooking for three minutes. Turn off heat.
Pour chicken on vegetables.

Serving suggestion:

Serve with Japanese white rice and Japanese green tea.

JAPANESE DINNERS

Chop Cher Dinner

Meat, vegetables and Japanese noodles (Dang Myan) dinner.
Serves four.

Ingredients:

2 pounds filet mignon (have sliced lengthwise in 1/4 inch slices at the market)
1 red pepper
1 pound pea pods
1 pound Japanese mushrooms, dry or fresh
2 bunches of spinach
1 bundle of carrots
1 package bamboo shoots
1 large onion
1 medium zucchini
1 package Dang Myan noodles
1 package steamed fish cake (Kamaboko), remove wood, cut fish cake in 1/4 inch slices
1/2 cup sesame seed oil
1 clove garlic, finely chopped
1 tablespoon fresh ginger, peeled and chopped
1/4 cup lite soy sauce
1 tablespoon toasted sesame seeds

Preparation:

Prepare the following vegetables and set aside: Wash, seed, and cut the red pepper in strips. Trim the tips from the pea pods. If dry Japanese mushrooms are used, wash, soak in warm water for 20 minutes, dry, and cut in strips. If fresh mushrooms are used, wash, dry, trim tips of stems, and cut in strips. Remove stems from spinach, wash, and cut in half. Wash, peel, and cut carrots in fine strips. Rinse bamboo shoots and cut in slices if not already cut. Finely chop the onion. Wash zucchini and cut in slices 1/4 inch thick. Cut the fish cake in thin slices and set aside. Cook the Dang Myan noodles according to package directions and set aside.

Heat 1/4 cup of sesame seed oil in a wok over medium heat for 2 - 3 minutes. Add the meat, garlic, and ginger and cook 3 - 4 minutes. Strain the meat over a bowl and set aside. Add the remaining sesame seed oil to the wok and heat. Add the cooked noodles and stir gently. Add the meat mixture, the vegetables that have been set aside, and the remaining soy sauce. Stir and toss to coat with the oil until heated through. Place on a warm serving platter and sprinkle with toasted sesame seed. A lite soy sauce may be provided for additional flavoring.

Serving suggestion:

Serve with miso soup and Japanese green tea. (See soup section for recipe.)

Japanese Style Meat and Vegetable Dinner

Serves four.
Wok cooking.

Ingredients :

1 - 2 pounds of lean, tender beef, pork, or chicken, sliced thin

Marinade:

1/2 cup teriyaki soy sauce
1/4 teaspoon ground ginger
1/4 teaspoon garlic salt
1 teaspoon toasted sesame seeds
1/8 teaspoon black pepper
1 tablespoon sesame seed oil
1 teaspoon brown sugar or natural honey
1 tablespoon Japanese sweet cooking rice wine
1 tablespoon sliced green onion, white and green parts separated
1/2 medium sized mild onion, sliced

Preparation:

Wash the meat and pat dry. Mix the marinade ingredients in a bowl. Add the meat to the marinade, cover, and refrigerate for three minutes.

Vegetables:

1 cup green onion tops, cut in 2 inch pieces
1 cup bamboo shoots, sliced in small pieces
1/2 cup fresh water chestnuts, rinsed and sliced
1 cup red pepper, seeds removed, cut in strips
2 cups French cut green beans
1 cup peeled carrots, sliced thin diagonally

JAPANESE DINNERS

1 cup broccoli florets
1 cup Japanese mushrooms (optional)

Preparation:

Wash and slice the vegetables. If using Japanese mushrooms, soak in one cup of lukewarm water for 30 - 40 minutes, dry, and slice in strips (remove hard center).

Ingredients:

1/3 cup sesame seed oil
1 tablespoon Japanese cooking wine

To cook:

Add sesame seed oil to the wok and heat over medium heat. Drain the meat. Sauté in the hot oil, stirring until lightly brown, about five minutes. Remove meat from wok, set aside, and keep warm. Add the vegetables to the wok, adding more oil if needed to coat the vegetables. Cook covered on high heat for five minutes. Lower the heat to medium and continue cooking, stirring occasionally, another five minutes. Add Japanese cooking wine and stir. Remove to a serving dish and flatten into a layer. Add the hot meat on top of the vegetables.

Serving suggestion:

Serve with Japanese rice cooked according to the package directions for two cups of rice.

Japanese Style Orange Roughy and Vegetables Dinner

Serves four.

1 gallon pot
1 large skillet

Ingredients:

2 pounds orange roughy fillets
1/2 cup rice wine vinegar
1 cup water
Juice of 1/2 lemon
1-1/2 celery stalks
1/2 cup small peas
1 large yellow pepper
1 large red pepper
1 bunch fresh spinach
1/2 cup fresh orange juice
1/3 cup sesame oil
1/4 teaspoon salt
1/4 teaspoon paprika
1/4 cup Japanese cooking wine
1/4 cup lite teriyaki sauce
1 tablespoon peeled and chopped ginger
1/2 cup fresh dill leaves
5 basil leaves
Soy sauce (served in small individual bowls)

Preparation:

Rinse fish in cold water, cut in four pieces. Pour vinegar and water in one gallon pot. Add lemon juice, celery, and fish to the pot. Cover and steam for three minutes. Remove fish from pot with a spatula. Set aside. Pour sesame oil in the large skillet. Wash red and green peppers, remove seeds, and cube the peppers. Place peppers and peas in the skillet. Heat and stir over medium heat for three minutes. Remove skillet from heat. Place fish on vegetables. Mix paprika, salt, pepper, ginger, teriyaki sauce, and wine in a mixing bowl. Pour sauce over the fish and vegetables. Wash spinach, pat dry, and remove stems. Put spinach on top of fish. Add the washed basil leaves and pour orange juice over all. Cover and heat on medium heat for three minutes. Sprinkle fresh dill over each serving. Serve with soy sauce on the side.

Serving suggestion:

Serve with white rice or "Japanese Red Beans and Rice." (See RICE section for recipe.) Serve with green tea.

Pork Tenderloin and Vegetable Wok Cooking Dinner

Serves four.

Ingredients:

2-1/2 pounds pork tenderloin
1 bunch celery
1 bunch carrots
1 bunch green onions
2 medium red peppers
3 garlic cloves
2 inches ginger
1/3 cup sesame oil
1/2 teaspoon salt
1 teaspoon black pepper
2 teaspoons roasted sesame seeds
1/4 cup Japanese cooking wine
1 tablespoon sake
1/4 cup lite soy sauce
1/3 cup teriyaki marinade and sauce

Preparation:

Wash tenderloin, pat dry, cut into 1/4 inch strips, place in a mixing bowl. Peel ginger and garlic, wash, pat dry, finely chop and add to meat. Add one tablespoon sesame oil and one teaspoon sesame seeds, salt, black pepper, wine, sake, lite soy sauce, and teriyaki marinade and sauce. Mix all together. Cover and refrigerate until ready to use.

JAPANESE DINNERS

Wash celery, carrots, red peppers, and green onions. Pat dry. Remove tops and bottoms from celery, diagonally slice. Peel carrots and slice diagonally. Cut red peppers into halves and remove seeds, julienne. Peel green onions and cut each into three pieces. Add 1/4 cup sesame oil to wok and heat on high. Use wooden spoon and stir while gradually adding carrots, celery, red peppers, onions, and sesame seeds. Cook two minutes. Place on warm serving plate, keep warm.

Place wok on high heat. Stir tenderloin into wok, cook for four minutes. Remove from heat. Pour over vegetables on serving plate.

Serving suggestions:

Serve with Japanese vegetable salad and green tea.

JAPANESE DINNERS

Salmon Dinner

Serves four.

Ingredients:

2 pounds salmon fillets (skin and small bones removed by butcher)
2 bunches fresh carrots with tops
2 bunches spinach
2 medium garlic cloves
1 inch ginger
1/3 cup teriyaki marinade and sauce
1/3 cup lite soy sauce
1/2 teaspoon black pepper
1/4 teaspoon salt
1/3 cup sesame oil
1 teaspoon roast sesame seeds
1 teaspoon brown sugar
5 basil leaves
1 tablespoon fresh dill
1 package fried bean curd
1/4 teaspoon white pepper

Preparation:

Rinse salmon in cold water, pat dry, and set aside. Use medium mixing bowl, add soy sauce, teriyaki sauce, sesame seeds, one tablespoon sesame oil, pepper, salt, and brown sugar. Peel and finely chop garlic and ginger, add to mixture. Wash basil in cold water, pat dry, chop and add to mix. Mix thoroughly. Lay salmon in oven pan. Pour prepared marinade sauce over salmon.

Place on bottom broiler rack. Leave door open one inch. Broil three to four minutes. Place salmon on serving platter. Pour sauce on salmon. Decorate with dill.

Remove veins from spinach, wash, pat dry, cut into three pieces, and add to one gallon pot. Add remaining sesame oil, stir, and cook on high heat for one minute. Remove from heat. Add diced fried bean curd, white pepper, and a pinch of salt. Mix well and place on a separate serving plate.

Serving suggestions:

Serve with Japanese red beans with rice and carrots. Always serve with Japanese green tea.

Shish-Kabob with Japanese Rice (Beef or Shrimp) Dinner

Serves four.
Preheat broiler for ten minutes.

Ingredients:

3 pounds filet mignon, wash and pat dry.
   Cut into squares.
If using shrimp, peel and remove the dark vein, wash, and pat dry.

Mix the following marinade:

1-1/2 tablespoon freshly peeled ginger, finely chopped
1 teaspoon toasted sesame seeds
1 tablespoon sesame seed oil
1/4 teaspoon white pepper
1 tablespoon sweet Japanese cooking rice wine
1 tablespoon lite soy sauce
1/4 cup teriyaki marinade and sauce
1/4 teaspoon salt
1 tablespoon natural honey

Preparation:

Add meat or shrimp to the marinade. Cover and refrigerate until ready to use.

Vegetables:

    1/2 pound small whole onions, skinned and washed
    1 pound of mushrooms, washed, dried, tips of stems trimmed
    1 large green pepper, washed, seeds removed, and quartered
    1 large red pepper, washed, seeded, quartered
    1 onion, washed, peeled, and quartered
    1 large tomato, washed, dried, and quartered
    4 small whole onion

Preparation:

Use bamboo skewers that have been soaked in water 20 minutes. Vegetable skewers: On each skewer place a slice of red pepper, a mushroom, onion, tomato, green pepper, and mushroom, finishing with a small whole onion. Meat only skewers: Thread four skewers with meat or shrimp only after draining marinade. Broil the meat or shrimp on the bottom of the preheated broiler tray for two minutes on each side leaving the broiler door open 1 - 1-1/2 inches while broiling. Set aside and keep warm. Broil the vegetables on the bottom of the broiler tray as for the meat two minutes on each side. Brush with pan juices and serve with the meat.

Serving suggestions:

Serve with lite soy sauce and Japanese rice. Serve Japanese green tea with Japanese dinners.

Shrimp Egg Roll Dinner

Serves four.

Ingredients:

2 pounds fresh medium shrimp
1/2 pound bean sprouts
1 bunch celery
1 package egg roll wrappers (20)
1 bunch green onions
1/4 cup sesame oil
2 egg yolks beaten
1 bunch carrots
1 inch fresh ginger
1 teaspoon black pepper
1/2 teaspoon salt
3 cups vegetable oil

Preparation:

Blanch bean sprouts in one cup boiling water for two minutes, chill in cold water, drain and pat dry. Wash celery, pat dry. Thinly slice two cups of celery, blanch in 1/2 cup boiling water for one minute. Chill with water, drain and pat dry. Remove carrot tops, peel and cut into thin strips, wash, pat dry. Using two cups carrots, blanch in 1/2 cup boiling water for one minute. Chill with cold water, drain, and pat dry. Peel and finely chop ginger, set aside. Trim onions, wash and pat dry, cut into 1/2 inch pieces, and set aside. Peel and devein shrimp, wash and pat dry. Cut shrimp into small pieces. Pour 1/4 cup sesame oil into 10 inch frying pan. Cook shrimp on high heat for three minutes. Remove shrimp from frying pan, using strainer to drain. In a large mixing bowl, place celery, carrots, bean sprouts, ginger, shrimp, green onions, one tablespoon sesame oil, black pepper, and salt. Using wooden spoon, toss to mix thoroughly, set aside.

Place egg roll wrapper on cutting board with one corner near you. Add about one-half cup of the above mixture. Brush beaten egg yolk on opposite corner and sides. Starting at corner near you, roll half way, fold sides in and roll tight. Place on wax paper, sealed side down. Add three cups of vegetable oil to 13 inch frying pan, heat on high. When hot add about five egg rolls to pan at a time. Turn egg rolls while cooking. Cook until egg rolls are medium brown on all sides. If heat is too high, reduce to medium. Remove egg rolls from pan and place on paper towels to drain oil from egg rolls.

Serving suggestions:

Serve with Japanese Vegetable Salad and Japanese green tea.

Shrimp Fried Rice Dinner

Serves four.
Use 14-inch wok for cooking.

Ingredients:

    2 pounds shrimp
    1 inch fresh ginger, peeled and finely chopped
    1 teaspoon sweet rice cooking wine
    1 tablespoon lite soy sauce
    1/4 cup teriyaki marinade and sauce
    1 teaspoon toasted sesame seeds
    1 tablespoon sesame oil
    2 cups Japanese rice
    1/2 cup carrots, peeled and cubed
    1/2 cup onions, cubed
    1/3 cup tiny peas
    Japanese soy sauce
    Sesame seeds or green onion tops for garnish

Preparation:

Make a marinade of the ginger, wine, soy sauce, teriyaki marinade and sauce, sesame seeds, and one tablespoon of sesame oil. Peel the shrimp, wash, and pat dry. Remove the dark vein down the back. Cut shrimp into small pieces. Place the shrimp in a bowl. Add the marinade, cover, and refrigerate until ready to use.

Cook the Japanese rice according to directions on the package, cool, and set aside. Heat one tablespoon of sesame oil in the wok over medium heat. Drain the shrimp and cook in the oil 3 - 4 minutes. Set aside. Stir fry the onions adding more oil, if needed, until brown. Remove from pan and set aside. Cook carrots, stirring, 3 - 4 minutes. Add another tablespoon of oil if needed. Put the rice and tiny peas in the wok. Toss as they heat. Add the shrimp, carrots and onions, carefully tossing all together until they are hot enough to serve. Sprinkle with sesame seeds and chopped green onion tops or chives for color. Transfer to a warm serving dish.

Serving suggestions:

Serve with soy sauce, Japanese green tea, and Miso soup.

Shrimp Tempura Dinner

Serves four.
Use wok to deep fat fry shrimp and vegetables.

Ingredients:

2 pounds shrimp
1 bundle asparagus
1 bundle carrots
2 sweet potatoes, medium size
Japanese tempura dipping sauce
1-1/2 cup tempura batter mix
Tempura soy sauce
1 quart vegetable oil
One ounce can of horseradish powder,
　　mix according to directions on can

Preparation:

Shell the shrimp, leaving the tails on. Cut shrimp to remove the black vein, wash shrimp. Wash the asparagus. Bend the stem at the base to break off the tough part and discard ends. Remove scales from the stems if desired. Peel the carrots, wash, and slice lengthwise in thin slices. Peel the sweet potatoes and slice lengthwise or quarter. Mix the tempura batter as directed on the package. Put the quart of oil in the wok. Heat on medium. Dip the shrimp and vegetables one at a time in the tempura batter. Cook in the hot oil until light brown.

Note: The Japanese have a separate bowl for each vegetable and the shrimp in front of the chef for easy dipping in batter and cooking.

Serving suggestion:
>Serve with one tablespoon of the horseradish powder mixed with water and stirred until very thick. Each person has a bowl of horseradish sauce and another for the Tempura dipping sauce.
>Serve with miso soup, Japanese rice, and Japanese green tea.

JAPANESE DINNERS

Shrimp Vegetable Dinner

Serves four.

Ingredients:

2 pounds medium size shrimp
1 celery stalk
1 bunch carrots
2 bunches fresh spinach
1 pound fresh mushrooms
1 inch fresh ginger
1 bunch green onions

1 tablespoon Japanese sweet cooking rice wine
1/2 cup sesame oil
1 teaspoon roasted sesame seeds
1/4 teaspoon salt
1/4 teaspoon black pepper

Preparation:

Peel shrimp, devein, rinse in cold water, pat dry, and store in the refrigerator. Remove tops and bottoms from celery, wash and pat dry, slice on bias, set aside. Remove tops and bottoms from carrots, peel, wash and pat dry. Slice on bias and cut into strips, set aside. Wash mushrooms and pat dry. Trim the bottoms and slice, set aside. Remove bottom stems from spinach, wash, and pat dry. Cut each leaf into half, set aside. Remove bottoms from green onions, wash and pat dry. Cut into three pieces and set aside. Peel ginger, wash, pat dry, slice, and set aside.

JAPANESE DINNERS

Heat 1/4 cup sesame oil in wok on medium heat. Increase heat to high and add vegetables a little at a time, stirring with a wooden spoon. Cook two to three minutes, stir in ginger, remove from heat, and pour onto serving plate; keep warm.

Add 1/4 cup sesame oil to wok, turn on high heat, add shrimp, sesame seeds, salt, and pepper. Cook for two minutes, remove from heat. Stir in cooking wine. Pour shrimp over vegetables.

Serving suggestions:

Serve with Japanese white rice and Japanese green tea.

Stuffed Japanese Brown Mushroom Dinner

Serves four.

Ingredients:

    2 pounds Japanese brown mushrooms
    1 pound boneless, skinless, chicken breasts
    1 pound large shrimp
    1/2 large white onion
    2 garlic cloves
    2 inches of ginger
    1 tablespoon Japanese cooking wine
    1 tablespoon flour
    1 cup lite soy sauce
    1/2 cup sake
    1/3 cup sugar
    1/2 teaspoon salt
    1/2 teaspoon white pepper
    1/4 cup sesame oil
    1 teaspoon roasted sesame seeds
    1 bunch parsley

Preparation:

Wash chicken, pat dry, remove fat, cut each breast into three pieces; place in a food processor. Peel shrimp, remove veins, wash, pat dry, and add to processor. Peel onion, garlic, and one inch of ginger; add to processor. Process until smooth and place in a mixing bowl. Stir in wine, salt, and pepper. Cover and refrigerate until ready to use.

Remove stems from mushrooms and discard. Wash caps in cold water, pat dry, and set aside.

Using medium size pot, add one tablespoon sesame oil, soy sauce, sake, sugar, and remaining piece of ginger, peeled and sliced. Heat on medium and cook while stirring until bubbles appear. Turn off heat and add sesame seeds. Set aside.

Stuff mushrooms with marinated chicken and shrimp. Sprinkle flour over stuffed mushrooms. Pour remaining sesame oil into a 13-inch frying pan and heat to medium. Add mushrooms; cover and cook for two minutes. Turn over mushrooms, cover and cook two additional minutes. Place mushrooms on a warm serving plate. Pour two tablespoons of soy sauce on top of mushrooms. Garnish with parsley. Serve remaning soy sauce in a side dish.

Serving suggestions:

Serve with Japanese white rice and spinach. Always serve with Japanese green tea.

Whitefish Dinner with Red and Yellow Peppers

Serves four.
Cook in broiler.

Ingredients for whitefish:

2 pounds fresh whitefish
1 tablespoon fresh ginger, peeled and finely chopped
1 tablespoon garlic, finely chopped
1/2 teaspoon black pepper
1 teaspoon toasted sesame seeds
1/3 cup teriyaki marinade and sauce
1/3 cup lite soy sauce
1 tablespoon sesame oil
Fresh dill for garnish
Lemon wedges for garnish

Preparation for fish:

Wash fish and pat dry. Mix the rest of the ingredients except dill and lemon. Heat the broiler for 10 minutes on broil. Place the fish and its sauce on the bottom of the heated broiler. Broil 6 - 8 minutes with the broiler lid open one inch. Remove fish to a warm serving plate. Pour juices from the broiler pan over the fish. Garnish with fresh dill and lemon wedges.

Ingredients for red and yellow peppers:

2 medium red peppers
1 large yellow pepper
1/2 cup vegetable oil

JAPANESE DINNERS

Preparation for red and yellow peppers:

Wash peppers, remove seeds, and cut into cubes. Heat oil in wok on high heat. Cook peppers in the oil, stirring, 2 - 3 minutes. Serve around fish.

Serving suggestions:

Serve with browned, cubed potatoes. (See vegetable section for recipe.) A salad may also be added with a bit of bib lettuce on each salad plate topped with two slices of tomato and one thin slice of red onion. Serve with petite croissants. Use salad dressing of choice.

Japanese Style Vegetable Dinner

Serves four.

12" frying pan
4 quart pan

Ingredients:

2 pounds whole green beans, tips removed
2-1/2 cups boiling water
2 tablespoon butter or vegetable oil
1 package tofu
Salt and pepper to taste
Toasted sesame seeds

Preparation:

Wash beans and arrange in orderly straight fashion in the frying pan. Pour 2-1/2 cups boiling water over the beans. Return to boiling. Cook 2 - 3 minutes using a spatula to turn beans. Do not cover. Drain and add one tablespoon of butter or vegetable oil and salt and pepper to taste.

Take tofu from package and rinse in cold water. Cut into three sections lengthwise. Dry with paper towels. Add one tablespoon of vegetable oil to the frying pan and heat at medium for 1 - 2 minutes. Cook the tofu in the oil, without stirring, for two minutes on each side. Remove from the pan to a cutting board and cut into cubes. Serve on a warm platter with the green beans in neat rows in the center surrounded by the tofu cubes. Sprinkle with toasted sesame seeds.

Sukiyaki Dinner

Cook in electric wok at 350 degrees.

Serves four.

Ingredients:

- 2 pounds beef loin, sliced thin (ask butcher to do this)
- 1 tablespoon fresh ginger, peeled and finely chopped
- 2 yellow onions, sliced thin
- 1/2 head of Chinese cabbage, washed and cut in 2 inch pieces
- 1 package tofu, rinsed and cut into cubes
- 1/4 pound mushrooms, washed and sliced with tips of stems trimmed
- 1 can bamboo shoots, rinsed and sliced thin
- 1 cup sukiyaki sauce
- 1/3 cup sesame oil
- 1 teaspoon toasted sesame seeds
- 1 5.2 ounce package Japanese noodles (Saifun)

Preparation:

Heat oil in electric wok at 350 degrees or cook on top of stove. Wash meat and pat dry, add to wok. Sauté meat until lightly browned. Add other ingredients, including the noodles, a little at a time. Add sukiyaki sauce. Toss and stir for 4 - 5 minutes. Sprinkle sesame seeds on top and serve.

Serving suggestion:

Serve with Japanese rice, miso soup, and green tea.

Japanese Soup and Vegetables

Miso Soup

Serves four.

Always served before Japanese dinner along with green tea.

Ingredients:

    5 cups of chicken stock
    1/3 cup of miso (soybean paste)
    1 package of hard tofu (soy bean curd)
    Chopped chives or green onion tops can be used as garnish, sprinkled on each serving of soup

Add the miso to the chicken stock and mix. Heat to boiling over medium heat, stirring constantly. Remove from heat. Remove tofu from package, rinse in cold water, and pat dry. Cut the tofu into half inch cubes. Add the tofu to the chicken stock. Heat over high heat about 5 minutes. Serve with a sprinkle of chopped chives or chopped green onion tops for garnish.

Bok Choy Vegetable

Serves four.

Ingredients:

4 - 5 pounds bok choy, wash and remove stems
1/3 cup Japanese lite soy sauce (low sodium)
1/4 cup sesame oil
1 teaspoon toasted sesame seeds
1/8 teaspoon salt
1/4 teaspoon black pepper

Preparation:

Buy bok choy from Japanese store. Mix soy sauce, sesame oil, sesame seeds, pepper, and salt. Add 4 cups of water to a two gallon pot. Cover and bring to a boil. Cut the bok choy into 1/4 inch pieces. Add to the boiling water, turning with a spatula. Turn off the heat and let stand one minute. Drain, rinse in cold water, drain, and pat dry. Add the bok choy to the soy sauce mixture. Stir, toss until mixed. Serve cold.

JAPANESE SOUP AND VEGETABLES

Japanese White Rice

Use matured, short-grain rice. Follow the directions on the package for making two cups of Japanese rice.

Japanese White Rice with Red Japanese Beans

1 cup of Japanese washed dark red beans
2 cups Japanese rice, washed

Cook beans only in two cups of water over medium heat. Simmer 45 minutes to an hour. Reserve water.

Add enough water to reserved water to make rice according to package directions. Add a bit of salt if desired. Cook the rice and beans together until the rice is done. The rice and beans should be the same color, dark red. Serve in small individual bowls.

Mixed Vegetables

Ingredients:

      1/4 cup sesame oil
      1/2 cup carrots cut lengthwise in strips
      1/2 cup pea pods, tips removed
      1/3 cup mushrooms, stems trimmed
      1/2 cup broccoli florets
      1/3 cup red sweet pepper cut in strips
      1 tablespoon Japanese sweet cooking rice wine

Preparation:

Heat the oil over medium heat in a wok. Add the vegetables and cook over high heat for 3 minutes, stirring constantly. Add one tablespoon of Japanese sweet cooking rice wine. Place vegetables in serving bowl.

Renkon (Lotus Root)

A Japanese vegetable that goes with all Japanese dinners and is decorative.

Serves four.

Ingredients:

2 packages fresh renkon (purchase at Japanese market)

Mix for sauce:

1 tablespoon lite soy sauce
1 tablespoon lite teriyaki marinade and sauce
1 teaspoon teriyaki regular marinade and sauce
1 teaspoon brown sugar
1/2 teaspoon toasted sesame seeds
1 tablespoon sesame seed oil

Preparation:

Open the packages of renkon and slice one-fourth inch thick, crosswise, to show the pattern. Bring 4 cups of water to a boil. Add the renkon. Simmer over low heat 15 minutes. Drain. Mix the sauce ingredients together. Pour the sauce over the renkon slices. Warm over low heat, turning carefully with a spatula often. Cook approximately 5 minutes and serve.

JAPANESE SOUP AND VEGETABLES

Yam Cakes

Serves four.

Ingredients:

2 packages yam cakes
1/4 teaspoon seasoned rice vinegar
1 teaspoon toasted sesame seeds
1/2 teaspoon sesame seed oil
1 green onion, finely chopped
1/4 cup lite teriyaki soy sauce

Preparation:

Purchase yam cakes from Japanese store already cooked. Remove from the package and rinse in cold water. Pat dry and cut into 1/8" x 3-1/2" slices. Mix the remainder of the ingredients and pour the sauce over the yam slices.

Serving suggestions:

Serve cold with Shrimp Tempura or Sushi dinner. (See Japanese Dinners section for recipes.)

Shrimp Vegetable Dinner
Page 52

Whitefish with Red and Yellow Peppers Dinner
Page 56

Barbecue Dinner
Page 75

Capon Dinner
Page 79

Golden Tilapia Fillets Dinner
Page 92

Leg of Lamb Dinner
Page 95

Red Snapper Dinner
Page 98

Salmon Dinner
Page 108

Chicken Fruit Salad
Page 154

New Potato Salad
Page 158

Tuna Salad
Page 166

Steamed Pears
Page 181

American Dinners

AMERICAN DINNERS

Barbecue Dinner

Serves four.

Ingredients:

    4 pounds baby pork ribs
    3 pounds beef skirt steak
    4 chicken breasts, bone in
    4 chicken thighs, bone in
    18 ounces barbecue sauce with honey
    1 pound package baby lima beans
    1/2 lemon
    1 tablespoon peppercorns
    2 stalks of celery cut in half
    Chives, chopped (optional)

Preparation:

Wash the meat and place in a pot of boiling water containing the celery stalks and freshly squeezed juice of half a lemon. Simmer 10 minutes, turn off the heat. Remove from heat. Barbecue meat over very hot coals for three to four minutes on each side. Brush the meat with barbecue sauce. Cook one minute more on each side. Cook the lima beans following directions on the package. Optional: garnish with chopped chives.

Baby Beef Liver

Serves four.

Ingredients:

    2 pounds of baby beef liver
    1/2 pound bacon
    1 large yellow onion
    1 pound mushrooms
    1/4 teaspoon white pepper
    3 tablespoons olive oil
    1 orange
    Pinch of salt

Preparation:

Wash liver and pat dry with paper towels. Place one tablespoon olive oil in a 13-inch skillet. Place on medium heat. Place liver in skillet. Sprinkle salt and pepper on liver. Cook about two minute per side or until proper color. Place liver in center of a warm oval serving platter and keep warm.

Peel and slice onion. Add one tablespoon olive oil to skillet, place on medium heat, place onions in skillet. Cook while stirring until golden brown, approximately three to four minutes. Place onions on serving platter beside liver.

Wash mushrooms, pat dry, trim stems and slice. Place one tablespoon olive oil in skillet. Place on medium heat. Place mushrooms in skillet, cook while stirring until light golden brown. Place mushrooms beside liver on serving platter. Cook bacon on medium heat until crisp, remove bacon and place on paper towels to remove all grease.

Place bacon on small serving plate. Decorate liver with orange slices.

Serving suggestions:
Serve with spinach, tomato slices, and white rice.

AMERICAN DINNERS

Beef Loaf Dinner

Serves four.

Use 9-1/4" x 5-1/4" x 2-3/4" loaf pan. Preheat oven for 10 minutes at 375°. Bake for 35 - 45 minutes.

Ingredients:

2 pounds very lean ground beef sirloin
1 egg
1/2 cup bread crumbs
1 tablespoon chopped parsley
1/2 cup low fat beef broth

Preparation:

Dampen fingers, then mix ingredients together and shape meat into loaf. Place in loaf pan. Bake 35 - 45 minutes. Let stand 10 minutes before slicing.

Serving suggestion:

Serve with sautéed tomato slices and baked cubed potatoes. (See Vegetables section for recipes.)

Capon Dinner

Serves four.

Preheat oven to 375° for 10 minutes. Roast capon 1-1/2 - 2 hours.

Ingredients:

6 pound capon
3 large cloves of garlic, finely chopped
1/4 teaspoon salt
1/8 teaspoon black pepper
1 tablespoon extra virgin olive oil
1 teaspoon extra light olive oil
1 tablespoon rosemary, crushed
1 medium onion, sliced

Preparation:

Wash capon and pat dry. Mix the rest of the ingredients together except the rosemary and onion. Rub the mixture both outside and inside the capon. Sprinkle crushed rosemary inside and out. Place the capon in the roasting pan and add the onion slices around the capon. Roast for 1-1/2 hours. Check for desired brown color. If not brown enough, continue roasting 15 - 30 minutes longer for desired color.

Serving suggestions:

Serve with halved baby new potatoes, acorn squash, and tiny peas. (See Vegetables section for recipes.)

Chicken Drumettes

Serves four

Ingredients:

    3 pounds chicken drumettes
    1 pound fresh mushrooms
    1 large yellow onion
    3 cloves garlic
    1 teaspoon ground paprika
    1/2 teaspoon salt
    1/2 teaspoon black pepper
    1 tablespoon flour
    1/4 cup olive oil
    1 bunch fresh parsley

Preparation:

Wash chicken and remove the skin, pat dry, and place in a mixing bowl. Peel and chop garlic. Add garlic, paprika, salt, pepper, and flour to chicken. Mix well and set aside.

Using a 10-inch skillet, pour in one tablespoon olive oil. Warm the skillet, add chicken, and cook on medium heat. Turn chicken to make sure chicken is brown on all sides. Place chicken on warm serving plate. Keep warm for serving.

Add one tablespoon olive oil to a 10-inch skillet and heat to medium. Peel and chop the onion, add to skillet, and cook until golden brown. Pour over chicken.

Wash mushrooms, pat dry, trim stems. Cut small ones into halves and large ones into three slices. Add one tablespoon olive oil to skillet and heat to medium. Place mushrooms in skillet, add more oil if needed. Cook, while stirring, until mushrooms are golden brown. Add pinch of salt and one-fourth teaspoon pepper. Place mushrooms around chicken on serving plate. Decorate with parsley.

Serving suggestions:

Serve with wild rice and green salad.

Chicken Vegetable Roll Dinner

Serves four.

Ingredients:

2 pounds skinless, boneless chicken breast
2 large red peppers
1 large yellow pepper
2 10-ounce packages fresh spinach
1 large onion
1/2 cup grated Parmesan cheese
Bread crumbs
1 bunch asparagus
1/2 teaspoon black pepper
1/4 cup olive oil
Pinch salt

Preparation:

Wash chicken in cold water, pat dry. Remove all fat from chicken. Place chicken breast on plastic wrap, cover with plastic wrap. Using meat tenderizer pound chicken until chicken is flat. Refrigerate until ready to use.

Wash peppers, pat dry. Cut peppers into halves, remove seeds and pulp, thinly slice and set aside. Wash spinach and pat dry. Remove large veins. Set aside.

Peel onion, wash and pat dry. Slice very thin, set aside. Remove hard bottom from asparagus, wash and pat dry. Place asparagus into hard boiling water for one minute, rinse in cold water, pat dry and set aside.

Place chicken pieces on cutting board. On each piece of chicken place three pieces of spinach and four thin slices red pepper. Put two thin slices of yellow pepper on the red pepper. Put one thin slice of onion on pepper, place two pieces of asparagus on onions. sprinkle parmesan cheese, black pepper, and pinch of salt on the vegetables. Roll into logs and tie each log. Roll each log in bread crumbs. Add one-fourth cup olive oil to a 13-inch fry pan and heat on medium until hot. Add logs and cook for two to three minutes on each side. They should be golden brown on all sides.

Serving suggestion:

Serve with applesauce and buttermilk biscuits.

Chicken Casserole Dinner

Serves four.

Preheat oven 350° for 10 minutes.

Ingredients:

2 12-ounce cans of chicken, solid white in water
1 cup bread crumbs
3 egg whites, beaten slightly
1/2 cup yellow onions, chopped
1/2 pound sliced mushrooms, washed, tips of stems removed
1/4 cup olive oil
Salt to taste
1 red pepper washed, seeded, cut in cubes (optional)

Preparation:

Oil a 7-inch casserole dish. Drain the chicken. Add the other ingredients and mix lightly. Place in a lightly oiled casserole dish. Put casserole dish in a pan half filled with hot water. Bake at 350° until set, approximately 40 - 45 minutes. Test with a toothpick. When done it will come out clean.

Serving suggestion:

Serve with a green salad and dinner rolls.

AMERICAN DINNERS

Chicken Dinner

Serves four.

Top of stove cooking: Use heavy 10" or 11" skillet.

Ingredients:

    4 chicken breasts, with or without the bone
    4 chicken thighs
    1 onion sliced
    2 garlic cloves, chopped
    1/4 cup vegetable oil
    1/2 teaspoon salt
    1/4 teaspoon pepper
    1/2 teaspoon paprika
    1 tablespoon white wine
    1 teaspoon lemon juice

Preparation:

    Wash the chicken and pat dry. Warm the vegetable oil in the skillet. Add the chicken, browning for about 3 minutes on each side over medium heat. Remove the chicken from the pan and keep warm. Brown the onion and garlic, move to the side of the pan. Add the seasonings and wine to the pan. Stir the lemon juice into the contents of the pan. Pour the hot sauce over the chicken. Heat as desired and serve.

Suggestion:

    Serve with brown rice, baby beets, and a green salad. (See Vegetables section for baby beets recipes.)

Fresh Ham Dinner

Serves four.

Ingredients:

3 pounds fresh bone-in ham
1 fresh pineapple
1/4 cup brown sugar
1 inch fresh ginger
12 cloves
6 ounce can sweet pineapple juice
Fresh parsley

Preparation:

Wash ham, pat dry with paper towels. Peel pineapple and slice. Place three pineapple slices in bottom of one 1-inch roasting pan. Place ham in the pan. Peel ginger and slice into three pieces. Stick ginger slices into ham. Stick cloves into ham. Pour six ounces pineapple juice over the ham. Rub one-fourth cup brown sugar in ham. Place two slices pineapple on ham. Preheat oven to 325 degrees. Place ham in the oven. Cook for 2-1/2 hours.

After one hour cooking time baste ham with juice from pan. Return pan to oven and continue cooking. Check to see if properly cooked. If not, continue cooking for additional 15 minutes.

Allow ham to cool for five minutes, slice ham and place on serving plate with the pineapple slices. Pour remaining juice over ham. Decorate with fresh parsley.

Serving suggestions:

Serve with sweet potato and your choice of brown rice or wild rice. Serve cranberry sauce and apple sauce in separate dishes. Serve with green salad.

Fresh Vegetable Deep Dish Pizza Dinner

Serves four.

Pizza Crust Ingredients:

    2 cups sifted flour
    1 teaspoon salt
    2/3 cup shortening
    1/2 cup cold water
    1/2 teaspoon butter or margarine
    1/2 teaspoon baking soda

Preparation:

Using a mixing bowl combine flour, salt, and soda. Cut in shortening with a pastry blender until mixture forms balls the size of small beans. Sprinkle one tablespoon of water over part of the mixture. Toss with fork and move to one side of bowl. Repeat until all mixture is moistened. Form into a ball. Flatten on lightly floured cutting board. Using rolling pin roll to a thickness of one-eighth inch. Lightly grease 13-inch skillet with butter or margarine. Fit pastry into skillet.

Filling Ingredients:

    1 pound mushrooms
    1 bunch carrots (with fresh green tops)
    1 bunch spinach
    1 large red pepper
    1 large white onion
    6 large fresh basil leaves
    1/2 cup grated Parmesan cheese

Preparation:

Rinse mushrooms in cold water, pat dry, trim the stem ends, slice and set aside. Remove tops and bottoms from carrots, peel, rinse in cold water, pat dry, julienne and set aside. Remove stems and veins from spinach, wash in cold water, pat dry, cut into three pieces, and set aside. Remove stem from pepper, cut into half and remove seeds, rinse in cold water, pat dry, julienne, and set aside. Remove top and bottom and peel onion. Rinse in cold water, pat dry, thinly slice and set aside. Rinse basil leaves in cold water, pat dry and set aside.

Sprinkle one tablespoon cheese on pastry. Spread a layer of carrots, spinach and onion over pastry. Sprinkle tablespoon cheese on vegetables. Spread red pepper on cheese, spread spinach on pepper, spread mushrooms on top of spinach, spread onions on mushrooms. Spread carrots on top of onions. Spread remaining spinach, mushrooms, red pepper and onions on mixture. Spread basil on onions. Sprinkle remaining cheese on top of basil. Cook in 400 degree preheated oven for 40 minutes. Test for doneness. Serve immediately.

Fresh Vegetable Stew

Serves four.

Ingredients:

1 cup pearled barley
1 pound large lima beans
1 stick celery
1 large white onion
1 bunch carrots
2 medium zucchini
1 lemon
6 basil leaves
2 medium tomatoes
1/4 cup white cooking wine
2 medium garlic cloves
1/4 cup olive oil
3 cups chicken broth
1/2 teaspoon pepper
1/2 teaspoon salt

Preparation:

Cook barley and lima beans following directions on packages. Remove top and bottom from celery, wash, pat dry, coarsely chop and set aside. Remove top and bottom from carrots, peel, wash, pat dry, dice, and set aside. Cut top and bottom from onion, peel, wash, pat dry, coarsely chop and set aside. Remove stem from zucchini, wash, pat dry, dice and set aside. Wash lemon and basil, pat dry and set aside. Wash tomatoes, pat dry, quarter and set aside. Peel garlic cloves, chop and set aside.

AMERICAN DINNERS

Using one gallon pot, add olive oil, place on medium heat. Add celery, garlic, and onions, use wooden spoon stir and cook until light golden brown. Add carrots, zucchini, stir and add lima beans, barley, basil, tomatoes, juice of lemon, and chicken broth, stir and cover. Cook on high heat for two minutes. Lower heat to low, cook for 15 to 20 minutes. Add salt, pepper, and cooking wine. Stir, cover, and cook for two minutes. Serve with petite dinner rolls.

Golden Tilapia Fillets Dinner

Serves four.

Ingredients:

    2 pounds tilapia fillets
    1-1/2 pounds baby red potatoes
    1 pound fresh mushrooms
    4 medium size red peppers
    2 lemons
    3 ounces fresh dill
    1 cup fresh orange juice
    1/4 stick margarine
    1/2 cup olive oil
    1/4 teaspoon black pepper
    1/2 teaspoon salt
    Ground paprika

Preparation:

Preheat broiler on broil. Rinse fish in cold water, pat dry, and place in refrigerator. Use a small mixing bowl, pour olive oil and orange juice into bowl. Add black pepper, salt, and one tablespoon fresh dill, mix well. Place fish in broiling pan, pour mixing over the fish. Slice margarine into eight slices and place on fish; sprinkle with paprika.

Place on second shelf in broiler. Leave door open one inch, broil three to four minutes. Check for desired color. Place fish on serving plate. Pour juices on top of fish. Decorate with dill and lemon slices. Keep warm until serving.

Wash red peppers and pat dry. Cut into halves, remove seeds and stem. Cut peppers into one-half inch cubes, set aside. Wash mushrooms, pat dry, remove stems, cut mushrooms into four pieces, set aside. Pour one-fourth cup olive oil into 13-inch fry pan. Place on medium heat. When oil is hot add peppers and mushrooms. Sauté two minutes while stirring, set aside.

Prepare new potatoes using recipe in Vegetables section. Place prepared potatoes, red peppers, and mushrooms on a serving plate.

Serving suggestion:
Serve fish and vegetables with petite croissants.

AMERICAN DINNERS

Fish Dinner

Serves four.

Use 9" x 13" x 2" baking dish.
Preheat oven 5 - 10 minutes on broil.

Ingredients:

2 pounds of fish of your choice
1 tablespoon extra light olive oil
1/2 cup extra virgin olive oil
1/2 cup freshly squeezed orange juice with the pulp
1-1/2 tablespoons freshly squeezed lemon juice
1/8 teaspoon black pepper
1/4 teaspoon salt
2 cloves freshly chopped garlic
1 inch piece fresh ginger, peeled, finely chopped
Dill for garnish

Mix all ingredients except fish and dill in a small mixing bowl. Wash fish and pat dry. Pour the mixed sauce over the fish. Place in baking dish. Place the dish on the bottom of the broiler pan. Put the broiler pan on the bottom of the broiler oven, leaving broiler door open 1 - 1-1/2 inches. Broil 7 - 8 minutes. Pour pan juices over the fish. Garnish with fresh or dry dill weed.

Serving suggestions:

Serve with rice or baby new potatoes in jackets, baby carrots, and steamed asparagus.
(See Vegetables section for recipes.)

Leg of Lamb (Boned) Dinner

Serves four.

Preheat oven to 325°. Roast 1-1/2 hours.

Ingredients:

3 pounds leg of lamb, boned by butcher
1 orange, halved
1 sweet yellow apple, cored and quartered
1 teaspoon honey
6 prunes, pitted
1/4 teaspoon rosemary, crushed
6 baking potatoes, peeled and rubbed with olive oil
Mint jelly

Preparation:

Wash and pat the meat dry. Wash the fruit and pat dry. Rub the inside of the cavity with the orange, leaving the orange inside. Add the honey to the core of the apple and place the apple in the cavity. Add the prunes to the cavity. Rub the rosemary on the outside of the lamb. Place the potatoes around the leg of lamb in a roasting pan and roast 1-1/2 hours. Check for desired doneness: 135° rare, 160° medium, 165° well done. Let the potatoes continue baking if not done. Let the roast stand 8 - 10 minutes before slicing. Fruit may be removed and served around meat or left inside. Arrange dinner on a warm serving plate. Serve with mint jelly.

Serving suggestions:

Serve with tiny peas and pearl onions, mixed. (See Vegetables section for recipes.)

AMERICAN DINNERS

Lobster Dinner

Serves four.

Ingredients:

    4 10-ounce lobster tails
    1 inch ginger
    1 large garlic clove
    1 cup olive oil
    1 tablespoon white cooking wine
    1 tablespoon parsley
    1/4 cup fresh lemon juice
    1/2 teaspoon black pepper
    1/4 teaspoon salt
    1 lemon

Preparation:

Split lobster tails open, wash well, and pat dry. Place in a mixing bowl. Add finely chopped parsley. Peel ginger and garlic, finely chop and add to mix. Add wine, lemon juice, pepper, olive oil and salt. Add lobsters to marinade and use tongs to turn lobsters to coat thoroughly. Place lobsters on an oven tray and put on bottom broiler rack leaving door open one inch. Broil two minutes and turn over lobsters. Brush on marinade sauce, cook additional two minutes. Place on serving plate and decorate with lemon slices.

Serving suggestion:

Serve with baked potato and green salad.

AMERICAN DINNERS

Pork Tenderloin with Sweet Potatoes Dinner

Serves four.

Use a 9" x 9 x 1-1/2" pan. Preheat oven 10 minutes to 325 degrees. Roasting for 35 - 40 minutes.

Ingredients:

    2 - 3 pounds pork tenderloin
    1 large garlic clove
    1 tablespoon vegetable oil
    1/2 teaspoon salt
    1 teaspoon crushed rosemary
    1 cup apple juice
    1/4 cup vegetable oil
    1/3 cup of honey
    4 medium sized sweet potatoes, peeled and quartered

Preparation:

Wash the meat and pat dry. Slice the garlic, insert into gashes made in the meat. Mix the vegetable oil and salt, rub into the meat. Sprinkle with the rosemary. Place the meat into the pan. Wash and peel the sweet potatoes. Cut into quarters. Mix the honey, apple juice, and vegetable oil, pour over the sweet potatoes. Put the sweet potatoes and the sauce around the meat and roast 35 - 40 minutes. Let rest five minutes before slicing.

Serving suggestion:

Serve with green beans or a vegetable of choice. (See Vegetables section for recipes.)

AMERICAN DINNERS

Red Snapper

Serves four.

Use 13-1/2" x 9-1/2" x 2" pan. Preheat broiler on broil for 10 minutes.

Ingredients:

    2 pounds red snapper fillets, cut into four serving pieces
    1/4 cup extra virgin olive oil
    1/4 cup extra light olive oil
    Juice of half a lemon
    1/4 cup fresh orange juice
    2 large cloves of garlic, finely chopped
    1/4 teaspoon salt
    1/2 teaspoon white or black pepper
    1 tablespoon fresh parsley, chopped

Preparation:

Wash the fish and pat dry. Put the fish in the baking dish. Mix the other ingredients and pour over the fish. Place the baking dish on the bottom of the broiler. Broil with the broiler top open 1 - 1-1/2 inches for 8 minutes (fish will be moist). Remove to a warm serving platter and pour pan juices over the fish.

Serving suggestion:

Serve with white rice and asparagus.
(See Vegetables section for recipe.)

Roast Beef Dinner

Serves four.

Use 9" x 13" x 2" pan. Preheat oven to 325 degrees. Roast meat 35 minutes. Cook to 140 degrees for rare and 160 degrees for medium.

Ingredients:

2 - 3 pounds beef roast, preferably tenderloin
1/4 cup extra light olive oil
1/4 teaspoon salt
1/8 teaspoon black pepper
2 cloves garlic sliced

Preparation:

Wash the meat and pat dry. Mix the olive oil, salt, and pepper. Rub the oil mixture into the meat. Slice the garlic, insert into gashes made in the meat. Roast uncovered at 325 degrees for 35 minutes. Test for doneness. If too rare, roast 5 - 10 minutes longer. Take from the oven. Let the roast rest 8 -10 minutes. Slice and serve in its own juice as a sauce.

Serving suggestions:

Serve with mashed potatoes or baked new potatoes, broccoli, and sautéed mushroom caps. (See Vegetables section for baked new potatoes and broccoli recipes.)

Roast Pork Tenderloin Dinner

Serves four.

Preheat oven to 350 degrees. Roast 35 - 40 minutes.

Ingredients:

 2 pounds pork tenderloin
 1 large clove of garlic
 1 tablespoon vegetable oil
 1/2 teaspoon salt
 1/2 teaspoon rosemary

Preparation:

Wash the meat and pat dry. Slice the garlic, insert into gashes made in the meat. Rub the meat with vegetable oil and salt. Sprinkle with crushed rosemary. Place in pan and roast 35 - 40 minutes until brown. Let rest 15 minutes. Slice and serve.

Serving suggestions:

Serve with wild rice and green beans.
(See Vegetables section for recipes.)

Salmon Casserole Dinner

Serves four.

Preheat oven to 350 degrees.

Ingredients:

    1 pound can sockeye salmon
    1 cup bread crumbs
    1 teaspoon salt
    1/2 teaspoon paprika
    1/4 cup olive oil
    3 egg whites, slightly beaten
    1 cup skim milk
    1 tablespoon chopped chives
    1 lemon, washed and quartered

Preparation:

Drain the salmon. Remove fat, bones, and skin. Flake the salmon with a fork. Set aside. Mix all the other ingredients except the lemon. Add the salmon to the mixture. Lightly oil a 7-inch casserole with olive oil. Place the salmon mixture in the casserole, pack lightly. Set the casserole in a pan of hot water about 2 inches high. Bake 40 minutes, test for doneness with a toothpick. If the toothpick doesn't come out clean, continue baking. Serve with a lemon quarter on each plate.

Service suggestions:

Serve with peeled, cooked baby carrots and a salad of bib lettuce, two cherry tomatoes, two hearts of palm, and three cooked oysters on each plate. Decorate with fresh dill. (See Vegetables section for baby carrots recipe.)

Scallops Dinner

Serves four.

Ingredients:

2 pounds jumbo sea scallops
2 7-ounce jars pickled whole baby corn
1 pound fresh mushrooms
1 bunch broccoli
1 ounce fresh ginger
1 large yellow onion
1/2 cup olive oil
1 tablespoon white wine
Pinch ground paprika
1/2 teaspoon black pepper
1/4 teaspoon salt
1 bunch green onions

Preparation:

Rinse scallops in cold water, pat dry. Refrigerate until ready to use. Peel yellow onion, cut into squares. Add one-fourth cup olive oil to 13-inch frying pan and heat to medium. Add onions, salt, and pepper. Cook for two to three minutes. Place on warm serving plate, keep warm. Rinse corn in cold water, pat dry. Using only the broccoli florets, rinse in cold water, pat dry. Add one tablespoon olive oil to 13-inch frying pan. Place on medium heat, add corn and broccoli, stir and cook two minutes. Peel and slice ginger, chop green onions, add to broccoli and corn. Add one tablespoon wine. Heat on high while stirring for one minute. Combine with onions and keep warm. Add one tablespoon olive oil to 13-inch frying pan, place on medium heat, add scallops. Cook for two to three minutes. Turn off heat. Using slotted spoon, place scallops on top of prepared vegetables. Sprinkle with ground paprika.

Serving suggestion:
Serve with white rice.

Shrimp Pasta Dinner

Serves four.

Ingredients:

2 pounds medium size shrimp
1 pound tagliatelle pasta
1 cup Parmesan grated cheese
1/4 cup margarine
1 tablespoon olive oil
1 cup skim milk
1/4 cup mixing flour
1 cup total, mix chopped parsley
Dill
Basil
Mint
1/4 teaspoon white pepper
1/2 teaspoon salt

Preparation:

Peel shrimp, devein, wash in cold water, and pat dry. Add shrimp to two cups boiling water. Cook on high heat for one minute. Rinse in cold water, pat dry. Refrigerate until ready to use.

Combine margarine and olive oil in a medium sauce pan. Melt margarine and add milk, flour, pepper, and salt. Place on low heat. Cook while constantly stirring until bubbling. If too thick, add one-third cup water. Stir and heat until right density. Add cheese and herbs. Continue stirring and simmer for two minutes. Taste and add seasoning if necessary. Add shrimp to sauce, set aside.

AMERICAN DINNERS

Cook pasta following directions on package. Place pasta on a warm serving plate. Pour sauce over pasta. Garnish with lemon slices and serve immediately.

Serving suggestion:

Serve with a green salad.

Spaghetti with Tomato Sauce Dinner

Serves four.

Use two gallon pot.

Sauce ingredients:

2 35-ounce cans Italian peeled tomatoes
1 6-ounce can tomato paste
2 large onions, chopped
4 cloves garlic, finely chopped
1 tablespoon Italian parsley, fresh or dried
4 large basil leaves, chopped fresh
1/4 cup extra virgin olive oil
1 tablespoon extra light olive oil
1 teaspoon salt
1 package Tagliatelle or other kind of spaghetti
Chopped parsley or basil (for garnish)
1 package grated Parmesan cheese

Sauce:

Warm the extra virgin olive oil in a medium size sauce pan. Sauté the parsley, garlic, basil, and onion to a light brown. Add the tomatoes and tomato paste. Heat, stirring constantly, until bubbling. Cover, lower the heat, and cook 45 minutes to one hour. Do not boil.

Spaghetti:

Add one gallon of water, the salt, and extra light olive oil to a two-gallon pot. Stir and heat to boiling. Add the spaghetti to the water and cook 6 minutes or according to package directions. Drain but do not rinse. Place spaghetti on warm serving plates. Pour tomato sauce over the spaghetti. Top with a sprinkle of chopped parsley or basil. Serve Parmesan cheese in a separate serving bowl.

Serving suggestions:

Serve with a green salad.

AMERICAN DINNERS

Salmon Dinner

Serves four.
Use 9" x 13" x 2" baking dish. Preheat oven to broil for 5 - 10 minutes.

Ingredients:

- 2 pounds salmon (other fish may be substituted)
- 1 teaspoon extra light olive oil
- 1/2 cup extra virgin olive oil
- 1/2 cup freshly squeezed orange juice, pulp and seeds removed
- 1-1/2 tablespoons fresh lemon juice
- 1/8 teaspoon black pepper
- 1/4 teaspoon salt
- 2 cloves garlic finely chopped
- 1 inch piece of fresh ginger, peeled and finely chopped
- 1 bunch dill weed (reserve four leaves for garnish)
- 1 lemon, quartered

Preparation:

Wash the fish and pat dry. Place in baking dish. Mix the rest of the other ingredients well and pour over the fish. Top with the dill weed. Place the dish on the bottom of the broiler oven, leaving the broiler door open 1 - 1-1/2 inches. Broil 7 - 8 minutes. When done, pour pan juices over the fish. Serve one quarter of the lemon and a dill leaf on each plate for garnish.

Serving suggestion:

Serve with baked baby new potatoes in jackets and baby carrots with asparagus spears for color. (See Vegetables section for recipes.)

Veal Cutlet Dinner

Serves four.

Ingredients:

    2 pounds veal cutlet, sliced thin by the butcher
    1-1/2 cups fine bread crumbs
    1 cup Italian Parmesan cheese, grated
    1 large garlic clove, chopped
    1 tablespoon extra light olive oil
    1 lemon, quartered
    3 eggs, beaten
    1 tablespoon parsley, chopped

Preparation:

    Wash veal cutlets and pat dry. Mix bread crumbs and cheese. Mix beaten egg, parsley, and garlic together. Lightly dip each cutlet in egg mixture. Dip in bread crumbs and Parmesan cheese mix coating lightly. Heat the olive oil in a frying pan on medium heat. Sauté cutlets 2 - 3 minutes on each side until light brown, adding more oil as needed. Serve one quarter of lemon on each plate.

Serving suggestion:

    Serve with spaghetti with tomato sauce and a romaine green salad.

Soups

Basic Chicken Stock

Use a 5-gallon pot. Cooking time is about 3 hours. Chill 3 hours overnight.

Ingredients:

5 pounds roasting chicken
2 stalks celery
1 large onion, cut in half
2 whole carrots, peeled
6 quarts of water

Preparation:

Wash all ingredients including the chicken and place in the pot. Add the water and heat to boiling over high heat. Cover partially and simmer until the meat falls off the bones, about 2 2-1/2 hours. Cool and then remove the vegetables. Strain the liquid through a sieve into a heat proof container and cool. Cover and refrigerate until the fat congeals at the top, preferably overnight. Skim the fat from the top. The stock can be refrigerated, covered, up to two days. When freezing, fill containers to within one-half inch of the top, cover, and freeze for up to six months. This stock is the basis for many soups.

Carrot Soup

Serves four.

Ingredients:

    4 cups carrots, washed, peeled, and sliced thin
    1 cup water
    1/4 teaspoons salt
    Pinch of white pepper
    1 tablespoon vegetable oil
    1 tablespoon flour
    1/2 cup skim milk
    4 cups chicken stock
    Dill or parsley chopped to sprinkle on soup when served

Preparation:

Steam the carrots in the water over low heat, covered, until tender. Drain the carrots. Add the oil to the carrots. Blend in a food processor until smooth, about one-fourth at a time. Return to the soup pot. Add the milk and flour that have been mixed until smooth. Add seasonings with the chicken stock and heat until desired thickness. If too thick, add chicken stock to thin. Sprinkle with chopped dill in winter and chopped parsley in summer.

Chicken Vegetable Soup

Serves four.

Ingredients:

3 boneless, skinless, chicken breasts, chopped
1 large onion, chopped
1/2 teaspoon salt
1/8 teaspoon black pepper
1/4 cup extra light olive oil
5 cups chicken stock
1 cup carrots, peeled and sliced thin crosswise
1 cup broccoli, chopped
1 cup green beans, cut in small pieces
1 cup celery, sliced thin

Preparation:

Other vegetables may be used if desired. Wash all vegetables and the chicken breasts. Pat dry. Warm the olive oil in a soup pot. Sauté the chicken breasts, onion, and seasonings until a light brown for about five minutes, stirring constantly. Add the chicken stock and vegetables. Bring to a simmer over low heat until vegetables are soft, about 10-15 minutes.

AMERICAN DINNERS

Corn Soup

Serves four.

Ingredients:

5 large ears of fresh corn or a 2 pound package of frozen cut corn
1/4 cup of vegetable oil
1/2 cup skim milk
1 tablespoon of flour
1/4 teaspoon salt
Pinch of white pepper
4 cups chicken stock

Preparation:

If using corn on the cob, wash the corn after removing husks. Fill a large pot with three quarts of water. Bring to a boil and add the ears of corn. Return to a boil and cook the corn 5-7 minutes. Drain, cool, and cut kernels from cobs.

If using frozen corn, cook according to package directions. Spin the corn in the food processor until smooth.

Put the vegetable oil, seasonings, and the corn in a soup pot. Blend the skim milk and flour until smooth and add to the soup pot. Stir in the chicken stock and blend together. Simmer, stirring until the desired thickness is reached, about 4 minutes. Garnish with chopped parsley before serving.

Fifteen Bean Soup

Serves four.

Ingredients:

1 package 15 bean soup mix
1 large onion, chopped
2 medium zucchini, sliced
2 medium tomatoes, quartered
2 cloves of garlic, finely chopped
1 tablespoon red wine
1 tablespoon capers
4 large basil leaves, left whole
2 cups chicken stock
Juice of 1 lemon

Preparation:

Carefully wash and sort the beans from any sediment and put in a pan. Cover with water and soak overnight. When ready to cook, drain the beans and put in a soup pot. Add two quarts of water and bring to a boil. Simmer slowly, uncovered, for 2-1/2 to 3 hours. Test to be sure the beans are cooked, then add the rest of the ingredients. Simmer for 30 minutes. Serve with a green salad and Sumiko's salad dressing. (See Sumiko's Special Salad Dressing under Lunch Salads section.)

Mushroom Soup

Serves four.

Ingredients:

1-1/2 pounds mushrooms, washed, tips of stems trimmed
1/4 cup vegetable oil
1 tablespoon butter
1 tablespoon flour
1/2 cup skim milk
1/4 teaspoon salt
Pinch of white pepper
5 cups chicken stock

Preparation:

Heat the vegetable oil and butter in a soup pot. Slice the mushrooms and stems and add to soup pot, stirring constantly until medium brown. Blend the flour and skim milk until smooth and add to soup mixture. Stir in the seasoning and chicken stock. Cook over medium heat, stirring constantly, 8 to 10 minutes. If too thick, add chicken stock as needed. Garnish with chopped chives or parsley.

Spinach Soup

Serves four.

Ingredients:

    4 - 5 bunches of spinach
    1/4 teaspoon salt
    1/8 teaspoon black pepper
    1 tablespoon vegetable oil
    1 tablespoon butter, melted
    1 tablespoon flour
    1/2 cup skim milk
    4 cups chicken stock

Preparation:

Wash the spinach after stems are removed. Using only water left on leaves, steam covered in the soup pot for one minute only in order to preserve the color. Rinse in cold water. Drain. Spin in food processor quickly, not to puree but to break into small pieces. Put vegetable oil in soup pot. Add the flour and stir with oil until smooth. Add skim milk and stir. Add spinach to soup pot with the seasonings. Add chicken stock, stir, and simmer over low heat 5 - 6 minutes or until desired thickness. If too thick, add more chicken stock. Garnish with chopped chives or chopped parsley.

Split Green Pea Soup

Serves four.

Ingredients:

    1 pound package of split green peas, washed
    1/4 cup vegetable oil
    1 tablespoon butter
    1 large onion sliced
    Pinch of white pepper
    1/2 teaspoon salt
    1 quart chicken stock
    1 tablespoon flour
    1/2 cup skim milk
    Paprika for garnish

Preparation:

Put the peas in the soup pot. Add the vegetable oil, butter, onion, salt, and pepper. Heat, stirring, while adding the chicken broth. Simmer over low heat until the peas are tender, about 30 minutes. Mix the flour and skim milk until smooth. Stir some of the hot peas into the flour mix to raise the temperature of the flour mixture. Add to the peas and cook, stirring, to the desired thickness. If greater smoothness is desired, spin a food processor a little at a time. Heat to serving temperature. Serve in soup bowls, sprinkling lightly with paprika for color.

American Vegetables

AMERICAN VEGETABLES

Acorn Squash

Serves four.

Ingredients:

2 acorn squash
4 tablespoon butter
4 tablespoon sugar or honey
Salt (optional)

Preparation:

Preheat oven to 400 degrees. Wash and cut squash in halves or quarters, if large, and remove seeds. Place cut sides down in two cups of cold water in a baking dish. Let sit one or two minutes. Turn upright. Place one tablespoon of butter and one tablespoon of sugar or honey to the hollowed-out center of each squash. Add salt, if desired. Bake 40 - 45 minutes.

AMERICAN VEGETABLES

American Brown Rice

Follow directions on a 14-ounce package. Use chicken broth instead of water for better flavor.

American Wild Rice

Follow directions on a 14-ounce package for four servings. Use chicken broth instead of water for better flavor.

Asparagus

Serves four.

Ingredients:

    2 bunches of asparagus or
        2 packages frozen asparagus
    2 tablespoons melted butter
    1/8 teaspoon salt (optional)

Preparation:

    If using fresh asparagus, wash the asparagus, break off the tough ends, and trim off the scales (if desired). Cover with boiling water and boil for two minutes. Remove while bright green. Pour melted butter over the asparagus and serve. Sprinkle with salt, if desired.

Asparagus Appetizer

Serves four.

Ingredients:

    1 loaf egg butter sliced bread, seedless
    2 bunches of asparagus
    1/2 cup light mayonnaise
    1/4 cup Dijon mustard
    1/4 teaspoon white pepper
    1/4 teaspoon sugar
    1 tablespoon olive oil

Preparation:

Cut bottoms off asparagus, using only top four inches. Peel asparagus. Put one cup water in cooking pot. Heat on high to boiling. Add asparagus, cook for one minute. Drain and rinse in cold water, pat dry, and refrigerate.

Mix mayonnaise with mustard, add white pepper and sugar. Mix and taste, add more sugar if desired. Cover and refrigerate.

Using a rolling pin, roll each slice of bread to a thickness of about one-eighth inch. Remove the crust, place bread on wax paper. Spread mayonnaise mustard mix on bread. Place one asparagus on each piece of bread and roll into a log. Place on a cookie sheet. Bake in preheated 375 degree oven for five minutes, check for light brown color. Brush olive oil on each roll and bake for one to two minutes. Cut each log into four pieces and serve.

Baby Beets

Serves four.

Ingredients:

2 bunches of beets
2 tablespoons melted butter
Chopped parsley

Preparation:

Cut off the tops of the beets (the leaves) and wash the beets. Put in a pan of boiling water, cover, and cook for 10 minutes. Lower heat and simmer 20 - 30 minutes. Test for softness. Drain and remove skins (they should slip off easily). Pour melted butter over the beets and sprinkle with chopped parsley. For large or medium sized beets, bring water to the simmering point. Boil for one hour. Remove the skin and quarter.

Baby Carrots

Serves four.

Ingredients:

2 pounds of fresh carrots or frozen carrots
2 tablespoons of butter, melted
Salt

Preparation:

Wash carrots and peel. If carrots are large, slice diagonally. Drop into boiling water and simmer two minutes. Test for desired tenderness. Drain. Pour melted butter over carrots and add salt.

AMERICAN VEGETABLES

Baby New Potatoes in Jackets

Serves four.

Ingredients:

2 pounds baby new potatoes
1/2 cup melted butter or olive oil
Parsley

Preparation:

Wash potatoes and remove blemishes. Cut larger potatoes in half. Cover with cold water. Bring to a boil over high heat. Reduce heat to medium and simmer, covered, until tender (about 10 - 15 minutes). Test for doneness. Pour melted butter over the potatoes and sprinkle with chopped parsley.

Baked Baby New Potatoes in Jackets

Serves four.

Ingredients:

    2 pounds baby new potatoes
    1/2 cup olive oil
    1/2 teaspoon salt
    1 sliced onion (optional)

Preparation:

Heat oven to 375 degrees. Wash potatoes thoroughly and remove blemishes. Quarter and place in an oven-proof baking dish. Mix olive oil, salt, and onion, if desired. Pour the oil mixture over the potatoes and stir. Bake on a cookie sheet or in a baking dish for 40 minutes. Test for doneness.

Baked Potatoes

Serves four.

Ingredients:

    4 large potatoes
    Olive oil

Preparation:

    Preheat oven to 400 degrees for 10 minutes. Wash and dry the potatoes. Rub with olive oil. Bake one hour.

Broccoli

Serves four.

Ingredients:

    2 bunches of broccoli
    1 tablespoon melted butter
    1/4 cup olive oil
    1/8 teaspoon salt
    1/2 cup water chestnuts, rinsed
    1 cup red sweet pepper, seeded and cut in strips

Preparation:

    Wash broccoli and use only the flowerets. Drop into boiling water and cook two minutes. Test for doneness. Remove from water while bright green. Mix melted butter and olive oil and pour over the broccoli. Add salt, if desired. Add water chestnuts and red pepper strips. Stir.

Brussels Sprouts

Serves four.

Ingredients:

    1 pound Brussels sprouts
    1/4 cup butter
    1/4 teaspoon salt
    Black pepper

Preparation:

Bring two cups of water to a boil. Add the Brussels sprouts and simmer 2 - 3 minutes. Drain and put in a serving bowl. Melt the butter and pour over the vegetables. Sprinkle with salt and pepper.

Green Beans

Serves four.

Ingredients:

    1 pound small baby green beans
    2 tablespoons melted butter or 1/4 olive oil
    1/4 teaspoon black pepper
    1/8 teaspoon salt

Preparation:

    Wash the beans and remove the tips. Cover with boiling water containing a pinch of salt. Simmer about two minutes. Remove from heat while still crisp and drain. Pour melted butter or olive oil over the beans and garnish with a pinch of black pepper.

Lima Beans

Serves four.

Ingredients:

1-1/2 - 2 pounds fresh or frozen lima beans
2 tablespoon melted butter

Preparation:

Drop beans into water and simmer until tender. Drain. Pour melted butter over beans and serve.

Oven Fried Potato Cubes

Serves four.

Preheat oven to 375 degrees.

Ingredients:

4 medium potatoes
1 teaspoon salt
1 tablesoon lemon juice
1/3 cup oil or melted butter

Preparation:

Wash and peel potatoes. Cut into desired sized cubes. Cover with water containing salt and lemon juice (to prevent discoloring). Set aside until ready to cook. Before cooking drain and pat dry. In a mixing bowl, blend the oil or melted butter and the salt. Toss the potato cubes in the oil until coated. Bake on a cookie sheet 10 - 15 minute or until done.

AMERICAN VEGETABLES

Pearl Onions

Serves four.

Ingredients:

    2 pounds pearl onions
    1/4 cup butter
    1/4 teaspoon salt
    Pinch of pepper

Preparation:

    Place onions in boiling water for three minutes. Rinse in cold water. Cut off the end of each onion and remove the skin. Place in serving dish. Melt the butter and pour over the onions. Sprinkle with the salt and pepper.

Peas

Serves four.

Ingredients:

1 pound package tiny peas or peas with pearl onions
1/4 cup melted butter
Pinch of salt
White pepper

Preparation:

Follow directions on the package. Do not over cook. Drain. Add melted butter, salt, and pepper.

Sweet Potatoes

Serves four.

Preheat oven to 350 degrees. Use 9" x 9" x 1-1/4" baking dish.

Ingredients:

3 large or 4 medium sweet potatoes
1/3 cup honey
1 cup apple juice
1/4 cup vegetable oil
Salt, if desired

Preparation:

Wash, peel, and quarter potatoes. Mix the honey, juice, and oil together. Add sweet potatoes to the baking dish and pour sauce over potatoes. Bake 30 - 45 minutes until brown.

Spinach Vegetable Dish

Serves four

Ingredients:

    3 bunches spinach
    1/4 cup olive oil
    1/4 teaspoon white pepper
    Pinch salt

Preparation:

Devein spinach, wash and pat dry. Use one gallon pot. Pour one-fourth cup olive oil into pot. Place on high heat. Add spinach, pepper, and salt. Cook for one minute while stirring with a wooden spoon. Remove from heat and place spinach on a serving plate.

Tomato Slices

Ingredients:

    4 medium tomatoes
    1-1/2 cups fine bread crumbs
    1 cup grated Parmesan cheese
    3 eggs
    1 tablespoon chopped parsley
    1 tablespoon olive oil
    1 tablespoon butter

Preparation:

Wash tomatoes and cut in one-half inch thick slices. Beat the eggs and add the parsley to the eggs. Mix the crumbs and cheese. Dip tomato slices in egg mixture. Coat the tomato slices with bread crumbs. Warm butter and olive oil in a frying pan. Cook the tomato slices at medium heat for three minutes on each side.

Serving suggestion:

Serve with "Veal Cutlets." (See American Dinners for recipe.)

Yellow Squash and Zucchini

Serves four.

Ingredients:

2 medium yellow squash
2 medium zucchini
1 cup bread crumbs
1/2 cup grated Parmesan cheese
1 tablespoon olive oil
Salt

Preparation:

Wash and dry the squash and zucchini. Rub with olive oil. Cut in half lengthwise. Sprinkle with bread crumbs and cheese on the cut side. Warm olive oil in frying pan. Sauté the vegetables on each side 3 - 4 minutes or until brown. Add salt to taste.

Lunch Salads

Sumiko's Special Salad Dressing

Serves four.

Ingredients:

- 1 tablespoon fresh lemon juice
- 1 tablespoon fresh cilantro or parsley, chopped
- 1 tablespoon fresh basil leaf, chopped
- 1 teaspoon garlic, freshly chopped
- 1 teaspoon powdered mustard
- 1/2 teaspoon black pepper
- 1/4 teaspoon salt
- 1 tablespoon sugar
- 1/2 cup extra virgin olive oil
- 1/3 cup seasoned gourmet rice vinegar

Preparation:

Mix ingredients thoroughly. Let the dressing stand at room temperature for 20 minutes. Shake before using.

Apple Salad with Squash

Preheat oven to 400 degrees.

Ingredients:

12 leaves of Swiss chard, washed and patted dry
2 medium sized red apples, cored and cubed
1/2 pound green grapes
1/2 pound red grapes
1 large pear, cored, peeled, quartered,
    and put in lemon water
4 small dark plums
1 large red plum, remove stone and quarter
1 bunch watercress, washed
2 kiwi fruit, washed, peeled, and sliced
1 large nectarine, remove stone and cut in quarters
1 lemon
1 tablespoon sugar
1 yellow squash, medium
4 tablespoons brown sugar
4 tablespoons butter

Apple Salad Preparation:

Wash and dry all ingredients. Mix two cups of water with the lemon and sugar and add apples to prevent discoloration. While the squash is baking, arrange the apple salad. On each salad place three leaves of Swiss chard. Arrange drained apple cubes in the center of the plate. Decorate each plate with four green grapes, four red grapes, a quarter of the pear, a quarter of the plum, kiwi slices, and a quarter of the nectarine around the apple. Decorate the top with water cress.

Squash preparation:

Cut the squash in half lengthwise. Place cut side down on a cookie sheet. Add 1/2 cup water. Bake for 45 minutes and test for doneness. Remove from oven. Cut each half in two pieces. Place on a small plate for each person. Put one tablespoon of brown sugar and one tablespoon of butter on each serving.

Serving suggestions:

Serve with hot buttermilk biscuits.

Broccoli Salad

Serves four.

Ingredients:

    1-1/2 pounds of broccoli, florets only
    2 small yellow tomatoes, washed and quartered
    2 small red tomatoes, washed and quartered
    2 eggs, hard boiled, cooled, peeled, halved
    4 pieces of hearts of palm,
        sliced diagonally lengthwise
    4 dark plums, washed and dried, stone removed,
        cut in half
    1 ripe nectarine, washed and dried, quartered
    12 celery stalks, washed and cut in 3 inch
        pieces lengthwise
    1 bunch of carrots, washed and cut into 3 inch
        pieces lengthwise
    12 bread and butter pickle chips
    1 medium mushroom, washed, dried, sliced into
        slices for each plate (uncooked)
    12 leaves of green leaf lettuce, washed and dried

Preparation:

Broccoli may be used raw or cooked. To cook, place in boiling water for two minutes. Drain and chill. Place three leaves of lettuce on each plate (not extending over the edge of the plate). Place three or four broccoli florets, depending on the size, in the center of each plate. Around the broccoli place one quarter of yellow tomato, one red tomato quarter, half a hard boiled egg, one piece hearts of palm, a dark plum, one quarter of the nectarine, celery sticks, carrot sticks, three pickle chips, and three mushroom slices.

LUNCH SALADS

Serving suggestion:
>Corn soup with crackers of choice.

LUNCH SALADS

Chicken Salad

Serves four.

Ingredients:

1-1/4 pounds skinless, boneless chicken breasts
1/3 cup low fat mayonnaise
1/4 cup celery, finely chopped
1/4 cup yellow onion, finely chopped
1 tablespoon lemon juice
1/4 teaspoon black pepper
1/4 teaspoon salt
1/4 teaspoon chopped fresh dill

Preparation:

Wash and dry the chicken. Put two cups of water in a medium pan, bring to a boil. Add the chicken and simmer over medium heat, covered for 15 minutes or until the chicken is done. Drain the chicken and rinse in cold water. Pat dry. Cut the chicken into one-half inch cubes. Mix with the above ingredients, cover and refrigerate.

Other ingredients:

12 leaves of red leaf lettuce, washed and patted dry
16 celery sticks, 2" x 1/4"
16 carrot sticks, 2" x 1/4"
1 yellow tomato, quartered
1 red tomato, quartered
2 small cucumbers, sliced thin diagonally
2 baby beets, cooked until soft, skinned and quartered
1 red onion, sliced very thin
12 black olives

Preparation:

On each luncheon plate place three lettuce leaves, two side-by-side and one across the bottom. Do not extend them beyond the plate. Press leaves against the plate. In the center place a scoop of chicken salad. Surround it with the celery and carrot sticks as the spokes of a wheel. Add a quarter of red and yellow tomato to each. Add cucumber slices, two quarters of baby beets, thin slices of red onion, and black olives for color accent.

Serving suggestion:

Serve "Sumiko's Special Salad Dressing" on the side with hot rolls or toasted English muffins.

Chicken Fruit Salad

Serves four.

Prepare chicken salad and chill. (See "Chicken Salad" recipe.)

Ingredients:

12 leaves of red leaf lettuce, washed and patted dry
1 green apple, cored and sliced very thin
2 small pears, peeled and cut in halves
1 peach, peeled and quartered
4 slices of honeydew melon, peeled
4 slices of cantaloupe peeled (or other yellow melon)
1 grapefruit, peeled and cut in 8 slices with the membrane removed
1 package raspberries
Walnut halves
Sprigs of fresh mint
Sumiko's salad dressing*
English muffins or other desired accompaniment

Preparation:

Arrange two leaves of lettuce side by side on each plate. Add one more at their base, keeping them inside the edge of the luncheon plate. In the center place a scoop of chicken salad. Surround the salad with slices of drained green apple, half a pear, a peach quarter, a slice of honeydew melon, a slice of yellow melon, and two slices of grapefruit. Sprinkle raspberries around the side where there is room. Add a few walnuts to each salad and decorate the chicken salad with a sprig of mint.

LUNCH SALADS

Note: Place fruit that may become discolored in one-half cup of lemon juice with one teaspoon of sugar.

Serving suggestion:

Serve Sumiko's Special Salad Dressing in a side dish. Serve with toasted English muffins or rolls of your choice.

LUNCH SALADS

Egg Salad

Serves four.

Salad ingredients:

1 dozen eggs
1/3 cup of celery, washed, dried, and finely chopped
1/4 cup yellow onion, chopped
1/4 cup mayonnaise
1 tablespoon fresh lemon juice
1/4 teaspoon salt
1/4 teaspoon black pepper
1 teaspoon gray mustard
1 tablespoon sweet pickle relish (or more if desired)

Preparation:

Cover the eggs with cold water and simmer for 25 minutes. Rinse in cold water and cool. Peel and chop eggs very fine. Mix the above ingredients in a mixing bowl and refrigerate.

Other ingredients:

12 green leaf lettuce leaves, washed and patted dry
12 slices of sweet pickle, drained
16 carrot sticks, two inches long
1 ripe tomato, washed and quartered
4 slices green honeydew melon
4 slices cantaloupe
4 slices watermelon
16 black ripe olives (seedless)
Dry red pepper for garnish
English muffins, toasted

LUNCH SALADS

Preparation:

On each luncheon plate place three lettuce leaves. Flatten against plate but do not extend past edge. In the center place a scoop of egg salad. Garnish each plate with three slices of pickle on one side, four sticks of carrots, and one quarter of the ripe tomato. Add one slice of each kind of melon to the plate and four ripe olives around the salad. Sprinkle the salad with red pepper for color. Serve with warm toasted English muffins.

LUNCH SALADS

New Red Potato Salad

Serves four.

Ingredients:

    Lettuce leaves, washed and patted dry
    1 large yellow pepper, washed, seeded, and cut in 3 inch strips
    4 large red peppers, washed, seeded, and stem end cut back 1 inch
    2 pounds baby new potatoes, washed, imperfections removed, boiled and sliced
    Salad dressing of choice
    1 medium red tomato, washed and quartered
    12 small French gherkins
    1 medium cantaloupe, washed, peeled, cut in 3 inch long slices
    16 3-inch carrot sticks
    1 celery stalk, washed, cut in 3-inch lengths, then into 12 sticks
    1 cucumber, washed, cut into 20 slices
    Chopped chives for garnish
    1 package red raspberries, gently washed and dried on paper towels
    Fresh mint for decoration

Preparation:

Place several lettuce leaves on each plate, keeping leaves inside the edge of the plate. Mix the potato slices with the salad dressing. Fill the red peppers with the potatoes and place one red pepper in the center of each plate. Around the pepper put five yellow pepper strips, one quarter tomato, three French gherkins, two slices of cantaloupe, four carrot sticks, four celery sticks, and five cucumber slices. Carefully sprinkle red raspberries over the salad as desired. Garnish with mint leaves.

Serving suggestion:

"Sumiko's Special Salad Dressing" may be lightly sprinkled over all if desired. Serve with spinach or carrot soup and crisp rice crackers.

Salmon Salad

Serves four.

Ingredients:

2 pounds salmon steak (have butcher cut in four pieces)
2 heads of Belgian endive
12 cherry tomatoes, halved
Hearts of palm, cut diagonally
1 bunch of asparagus, peeled, boiled 2 minutes, and chilled
1 bunch watercress
8 French gherkins
3 lemons
12 pea pods, boiled 2 minutes, rinsed in cold water, dried
4 slices watermelon
1 pear, peeled and quartered
1 small fig, cut in quarters
1 red onion, sliced thin
Chives, chopped
Sumiko's Special Salad Dressing
Croissants

Preparation:

Steam the salmon in two cups of boiling water and one-third cup of lemon juice for 6 - 8 minutes. Drain and refrigerate. Remove skin and bones. Mix two cups of water, one tablespoon sugar, and one-half cup lemon juice. Cut the stems of the endive and dip leaves in sugar/lemon mixture. Remove leaves and dry.

LUNCH SALADS

Place several leaves of endive on each luncheon plate. Do not extend leaves past edges of plates. Place a salmon steak in the center of the plate. Add six tomato halves and one-half of palm to each plate. Place an asparagus tip, cut to three inches in length, on the endive. Add two French gherkins, one quarter of a lemon, three pea pods, and two slices of watermelon two inches long. Add one quarter of the pear and fig on the plate. Top with the salmon and thin red onion slices. Garnish with chopped chives.

Serve "Sumiko's Special Salad Dressing" on the side.

Serving suggestion:

Warm petite croissants could be served with the salad.

Shrimp Vegetable Salad

Serves four.

Ingredients:

    1 pound medium sized shrimp
    1 lemon
    1 medium red tomato
    12 small French gherkins
    1 large yellow pepper, washed, seeded, cut in 3 inch strips
    4 large red peppers, seeded, 1 inch cut off stem end
    2 pounds tiny red potatoes, washed and boiled
    1 medium sized cantaloupe, cut into 3 inch long slices
    1 carrot, washed, cut into 3 inch sticks
    1 celery stalk, washed, cut into 3 inch sticks
    1 medium sized cucumbers, peeled, cut into 20 slices
    Fresh mint for garnish
    12 Romaine lettuce leaves, washed and dried
    Chopped chives for garnish and flavor

Preparation:

Clean and devein shrimp. Boil shrimp in two cups of water for two minutes. Remove and cool with cold water. Pat dry. Boil the tiny red potatoes. Slice and stuff into the hollow red peppers.

Arrange the following on luncheon plates:

LUNCH SALADS

Place three Romaine leaves on each plate, not over the edges of the plate. Divide the shrimp on to the center of the plates around the stuffed red pepper. Add a quarter of the lemon. Surround with a red tomato quarter, French gherkins, strips of yellow pepper, carrot strips, four celery sticks, five slices of cucumber, and three slices of cantaloupe.

Serving suggestion:

Serve with spinach soup and crisp rice crackers or warm petite dinner rolls.

Spinach Salad

Serves four.

Ingredients:

    2 10-ounce bunches of fresh spinach, washed and dried
    1 red onion, sliced thin
    1 pound of bacon, cooked and drained on paper towels, then crushed
    Walnut pieces

Preparation:

    Remove stems and center lines of the spinach leaves. Top with bacon onion bits. Add slices of onion on top of the spinach. Sprinkle walnut pieces over all. Use "Sumiko's Special Salad Dressing" over the salad.

Serving suggestions:

    Serve with mushroom soup and sesame thin wheat crackers.

LUNCH SALADS

Vegetable Salad

Serves four.

Ingredients:

1 bunch celery
1 package carrots
1 medium cucumber
1 medium red onion
4 medium zucchini
1/2 cup extra virgin olive oil
1 tablespoon roasted sesame seeds
1/2 cup rice vinegar
1 teaspoon black pepper
1/2 teaspoon salt
1/2 teaspoon sugar
1-1/2 inches fresh ginger

Preparation:

Cut tops and bottoms from celery, zucchini and carrots. Peel carrots and onion. Use large mixing bowl. Split celery, carrots, zucchini and cucumber into halves, and cut into cubes. Cube onion, place vegetables in the mixing bowl. Add olive oil, rice vinegar, sesame seeds, black pepper, salt, and sugar to bowl. Peel ginger, slice and add to bowl. Using wooden spoon, toss salad. Place in a small bowl, cover, and refrigerate until ready to serve.

Tuna Salad

Serves four.

13" shallow pan with cover.

Ingredients:

    2 pounds fresh tuna, washed, dried, and cut into 4 servings
    celery
    2 lemons
    1 bunch red lettuce (12 leaves)
    2 small cucumber, cut into 12 slices
    1 bunch carrots, cut into 12 3" sticks
    1 can lichees (12 pieces)
    12 black olives
    12 slices fruit (orange, apricot, pear or pineapple)
    12 slices sweet pickle (optional)
    Basil leaves
    Petite rolls or crackers
    Salad dressing

Preparation:

Place tuna in shallow pan. Add two cups of water with one tablespoon juice from lemon. Add one stick of celery, broken in half. Cover and steam 2 - 3 minutes. Remove with a spatula to cool until cold.

LUNCH SALADS

On salad plate place three lettuce leaves, washed and dried, and one serving of tuna in the center of the plate. Around the tuna on each plate place three or four slices of small cucumber, three carrot sticks, three pieces lychees, three pieces of fruit, three black olives, and three slices of sweet pickle (optional). Garnish tuna with basil leaves and a lemon wedge on the side. Use salad dressing of choice. Serve with the rolls or crackers.

Desserts

DESSERTS – LIGHT AND QUICK

Applesauce

Ingredients:

      6 pounds Jonathan apples
      5 cinnamon sticks
      1 teaspoon ground cinnamon
      1 cup sugar

Preparation:

Peel apples and remove the cores. Cut apples into quarters. Rinse in cold water, pat dry with a cloth. Place apples in a two-gallon pot. Place cinnamon sticks in a small sauce pan, add 1-2/3 cups water. Place on high heat, bring to a boil. Simmer for 30 minutes. Pour through a very fine strainer into cooker. Use wooden spoon and stir to mix cinnamon water with apples. Cover and cook on high heat until steaming. Turn off heat. Add one teaspoon ground cinnamon and one cup sugar. Mix all ingredients, place on medium heat for 20 minutes, turn off heat. Use a wooden spoon to stir to break apple pieces into smaller pieces. Cover and simmer for ten to fifteen minutes. Taste to determine proper taste. If more sugar is needed, add one-half cup sugar and simmer an additional five to eight minutes.

DESSERTS – LIGHT AND QUICK

Baked Apples

Serves four.

Bake at 375° for 40 - 60 minutes.

Ingredients:

4 Rome Beauty apples, washed and cored
8 pats of butter
Brown sugar
Cinnamon

Preparation:

Peel the top third of the apples and place in a shallow baking dish. In the empty center of each apple place one pat of butter, fill with brown sugar, and place another pat of butter on top. Sprinkle with cinnamon. Add one-half cup water in baking dish and bake at 375 degrees until soft, approximately 40 - 60 minutes. Baste with any juice in baking dish.

Baked Peaches

Ingredients:

    Canned peach halves
    Maple syrup
    Brandy (optional)

In a shallow baking dish place desired number of peach halves. Fill each peach hollow with maple syrup. Heat in oven at 300 degrees until warm. Pour 1 - 2 teaspoons of brandy over each peach, if desired.

DESSERTS – LIGHT AND QUICK

Fresh Baked Apple Pie

Pastry Ingredients:

    2 cups sifted flour
    1 teaspoon salt
    2/3 cup shortening
    1/2 cup cold water
    1/2 teaspoon butter or margarine
    2 teaspoons sugar

Preparation:

Using a mixing bowl, add flour, sugar and salt. Cut in shortening with pastry blender until pieces are the size of small beans. Sprinkle one tablespoon water over part of the mixture. Gently toss with fork and push to one side of bowl. Repeat until all mixture is moistened. Form into a ball. Divide into two pieces. Flatten on lightly floured surface by pressing with edge of hand. Using a rolling pin, roll from center to edge until one-eighth inch thick. Using butter or margarine, lightly grease nine-inch pie pan. Fit pastry in pie pan. Prepare top crust the same way as the lower crust.

Filling Ingredients:

    5 pounds Jonathan apples
    1/2 cup brown sugar
    1/2 teaspoon cinnamon
    1 teaspoon vanilla
    2 tablespoons butter or margarine
    2 tablespoons all purpose flour

DESSERTS – LIGHT AND QUICK

Preparation:

Peel and core apples, wash and pat dry. Slice into eight pieces. Combine sugar, flour, spices and dash of salt; mix with apples. Fill previously prepared pie pan with mixture, dot with butter. Place top crust on pie filling, trim crust to edge of pie pan. Cut slits for escape of steam. Use a fork to seal edge around pan. Preheat oven to 400 degrees and bake for 50 minutes or until done.

Serving suggestions:

Serve with ice cream or whipped cream.

Fresh Cranberry Sauce

Ingredients:

    12 ounces fresh cranberries
    1 large lemon
    1-1/2 cups sugar
    1-1/2 cups water

Preparation:

Place sugar and water in a one-half gallon sauce pan. Cook on medium heat for five minutes. Wash cranberries, pat dry. Add cranberries to sugar and water sauce. Using a medium grater, grate one teaspoon lemon rind and add to cranberries. Simmer until skins pop open, approximately five minutes. Remove from heat and cool in saucepan.

DESSERTS – LIGHT AND QUICK

Fresh Fruit and Jell-O® Mold

Dessert for four.

Ingredients:

    6 ounce box of cherry Jell-O® gelatin
    2 Mandarin oranges
    2 medium freestone peaches
    1/2 pound strawberries

Preparation:

    Peel Mandarin oranges, break into pieces, set aside. Place peaches in two cups boiling water for one to two minutes. Remove and peel, cut into half, remove pit, slice into eight pieces, and set aside. Wash strawberries, pat dry and remove stems, place in refrigerator until ready to use. Pour Jell-O® into mixing bowl. Pour two cups boiling water over Jell-O®, stir with spoon until smooth. Stir oranges and peaches into Jell-O®. Pour into nine inch Jell-O® mold, place in refrigerator for two hours. Using a thin knife, separate Jell-O® from mold. Invert a serving plate over the Jell-O®, turn over and remove mold. Decorate with strawberries, serve with whipping cream.

Fresh Fruit Dessert

Ingredients:

    Fresh fruit
1 can frozen lemonade, thawed, undiluted
1/2 cup brandy (or less, if desired)
2 tablespoons of honey

Preparation:

    Prepare fruit* of choice as desired (melon balls, slices, cubes, etc.). Mix the lemonade, brandy, and honey. Marinate the fruit in the sauce until chilled or longer if time allows. Arrange and serve as desired.

*Note: Particularly good on honeydew melon.

DESSERTS – LIGHT AND QUICK

Ice Cream, Peanut Butter and Honey Graham Cracker Dessert

Serves four.

Ingredients:

- 1/2 gallon vanilla ice cream
- 1 pound box honey graham crackers
- 14 ounce jar creamy peanut butter
- 1 bunch fresh mint

Preparation:

Spread wax paper on cutting board. Using a rolling pin, finely crush graham crackers to make four cups. Using a large mixing bowl, mix two cups of graham cracker crumbs, 1-1/2 cups peanut butter, and three cups ice cream. Make into tennis size balls. Coat balls with remaining graham cracker crumbs. Place in freezer until ready to serve. Place on serving plate with a sprig of fresh mint on each ball for decoration.

DESSERTS – LIGHT AND QUICK

Oatmeal Raisin Cookies

Ingredients:

    2 cups one-minute oatmeal
    1 cup baking raisins
    1/2 teaspoon baking soda
    1/2 cup shortening
    1/2 cup butter
    2 cups flour
    1 egg
    1 teaspoon cinnamon
    1 teaspoon vanilla
    1/2 teaspoon salt
    1/4 cup skim milk
    1 cup brown sugar

Preparation:

    Cut raisins into small pieces. Place raisins, flour, and oatmeal in a mixing bowl, set aside. Using another mixing bowl, add shortening, butter, brown sugar, cinnamon, egg, baking soda, vanilla, salt, and skim milk. Using blender, blend until very smooth. Add flour, raisins, and oatmeal to mixture and blend. Place one tablespoon of batter for each cookie on a cookie sheet. Leave space between each cookie. Use a spoon to flatten cookie. Preheat oven to 375 degrees. Bake for 11 to 12 minutes. Remove from oven. Cool one minute, then remove cookies from sheet.

Steamed Pears

Serves four.

Ingredients:
4 brown pears with stems

Preparation:
Steam, covered, on a rack in a small amount of water for 8 - 10 minutes. Wash in cold water, cool, and gently peel, keeping stems on. Chill, covered, in refrigerator until ready to glaze.

Note: The pears may be prepared a day in advance.

Glaze:
1 cup water
1/2 cup sugar
1 1/2 stick cinnamon
Orange liqueur

Preparation:
Add the sugar to the water and stir until dissolved. Add the cinnamon sticks and cook over low heat for 10 minutes. Cool. Remove cinnamon stick. Pour glaze over pears and refrigerate, covered, stem up.

When ready to serve, warm pears enough to soften the glaze. Spoon glaze over pears until all the glaze is used. Use a spatula to carefully lift each pear, stem up, onto a serving plate. Slowly pour 1 - 2 teaspoons of orange liqueur over each pear.

Stewed Fresh Fruit

Syrup:

2 cups water
1 cup sugar

Preparation:

Cook water and sugar until syrup consistency. While hot add desired fruit combinations. Cook until tender.

Note: The fruit juice can be flavored, as desired, with lemon, cinnamon, wine, or mint, and chilled over the fruit. These seasonings can be used in canned fruit juices also.

Index to Recipes

Acorn Squash
    123
American Brown Rice
    124
American Wild Rice
    125
Asparagus
    126
Asparagus Appetizer
    127
Apple Salad with Squash
    148-149
Applesauce
    171
Baby Beef Liver Dinner
    76-77
Baby Beets
    128
Baby Carrots
    129
Baby New Potatoes in Jackets
    130
Baked Apples
    172
Baked Baby New Potatoes in Jackets
    131
Baked Peaches
    173
Baked Potatoes
    132
Barbecue Dinner
    75

Basic Chicken Stock Soup
   113
Beef Loaf Dinner
   78
Beef Teriyaki Dinner
   30
Bok-Choy Vegetable
   64
Broccoli
   133
Broccoli Salad
   150-151
Brussels Sprouts
   134
Capon Dinner
   79
Carrot Soup
   114
Chicken Dinner
   85
Chicken and Vegetable Stir Fry Dinner
   32-33
Chicken Casserole Dinner
   84
Chicken Drumettes Dinner
   80-81
Chicken Salad
   152-153
Chicken Fruit Salad
   154-155
Chicken Teriyaki with Vegetable and Rice Dinner
   31
Chicken Vegetable Roll Dinner
   82-83

Chicken Vegetable Soup
　115
Chop Cher Dinner
　34-35
Corn Soup
　116
Egg Salad
　156-157
Fifteen Bean Soup
　117
Fish Dinner
　94
Fresh Baked Apple Pie
　174-175
Fresh Cranberry Sauce
　176
Fresh Fruit Dessert
　178
Fresh Fruit and Jell-O® Mold
　177
Fresh Ham Dinner
　86-87
Fresh Vegetable Deep Dish Pizza Dinner
　88-89
Fresh Vegetable Stew Dinner
　90-91
Golden Tilapia Fillets Dinner
　92-93
Green Beans
　135
Ice Cream, Peanut Butter and Graham Cracker Dessert
　179
Japanese Style Meat and Vegetable Dinner
　36-37

Japanese Style Orange Roughy and Vegetables Dinner
    38-39
Japanese Style Vegetable Dinner
    58
Japanese White Rice
    65
Japanese White Rice with Red Japanese Beans
    66
Leg of Lamb (Boned) Dinner
    95
Lima Beans
    136
Lobster Dinner
    96
Miso Soup
    63
Mixed Vegetables (Japanese)
    67
Mushroom Soup
    118
New Red Potato Salad
    158-159
Oatmeal Raisin Cookies
    180
Oven Fried Potato Cubes
    137
Pearl Onions
    138
Peas
    139
Pork Tenderloin and Vegetable Wok Cooking Dinner
    40-41
Pork Tenderloin with Sweet Potatoes Dinner
    97

Red Snapper Dinner
  98
Roast Beef Dinner
  99
Roast Pork Tenderloin Dinner
  100
Renkon (Lotus Root)
  68
Salmon Dinner
  108
Salmon Dinner (Japanese)
  42-43
Salmon Casserole Dinner
  101
Salmon Salad
  160-161
Scallops Dinner
  102-103
Shish-Kabob with Japanese Rice (Beef or Shrimp) Dinner
  44-45
Shrimp Egg Roll Dinner
  46-47
Shrimp Fried Rice Dinner
  48-49
Shrimp Pasta Dinner
  104-105
Shrimp Tempura Dinner
  50-51
Shrimp Vegetable Dinner
  52-53
Shrimp Vegetable Salad
  162-163
Spaghetti with Tomato Sauce Dinner
  106-107

Spinach Salad
  164
Spinach Soup
  119
Spinach Vegetable Dish
  141
Split Green Pea Soup
  120
Steamed Pears
  181
Stewed Fresh Fruit
  182
Stuffed Japanese Brown Mushroom Dinner
  54-55
Sukiyaki Dinner
  59
Sumiko's Special Salad Dressing
  147
Sushi
  27-29
Sweet Potatoes
  140
Tomato Slices
  142
Tuna Salad
  166-167
Veal Cutlet Dinner
  109
Vegetable Salad
  165
Whitefish Dinner with Red and Yellow Peppers
  56-57
Yam Cakes
  69
Yellow Squash and Zucchini
  143

Order form

Mail Orders:
Triangle Park Press
P.O. Box #335
Lake Bluff, IL 60044
Fax Orders   847-615-2425
Phone Orders 847-615-8326

Please send the following books:

Quantity	Title	Each	Total
	Japanese, High-Style Cooking	$16.95	

Shipping and handling free.

Payment: ☐ Check   ☐ MasterCard   ☐ Visa
(Make checks payable to Triangle Park Press)

Card Number: _____

Name on card: _____

Exp. Date: _____

Ship to: _____

_____

_____

Telephone number: _____

This page may be photocopied.